West African Governments and Volunteer Development Organizations

Priorities for Partnership

Dr. Willard R. Johnson
The Massachusetts Institute of Technology

Dr. Vivian R. Johnson
Boston University

UNIVERSITY
PRESS OF
AMERICA

Lanham • New York • London

Copyright © 1990 by

University Press of America®, Inc.

4720 Boston Way
Lanham, Maryland 20706

3 Henrietta Street
London WC2E 8LU England

Library of Congress Cataloging-in-Publication Data

Johnson, Willard R., 1935–   .
West African governments and volunteer development organizations :
priorities for partnership / by Willard R. Johnson and Vivian R. Johnson.
          p.   cm.
Includes bibliographical references.
1. Non-governmental organizations—Africa, West.   2. Economic
assistance—Africa, West.   3. Technical assistance—Africa, West.
          I. Johnson, Vivian R., 1935–   .   II. Title.
HC1000.J64   1989   338.9'1'0966—dc20   89–39288 CIP

ISBN 0–8191–7746–6 (alk. paper)
ISBN 0–8191–7747–4 (pbk. : alk. paper)

DEDICATION

We dedicate this work to the leaders of African volunteer development organizations, and especially to the members and leaders of the Federation of African Volunteer Development Organizations, whose common mission is of crucial significance to the future well-being of Africa and her peoples, where-ever they are.

ACKNOWLEDGEMENT

The authors are extremely grateful to the Fulbright Fellowship Program for the award of a West Africa Regional Senior Research Fellowship in 1987, which permitted the field research for this study.

We are also extremely grateful to the Rockefeller Foundation Study Center at Bellagio, Italy, where the draft report was written.

The M.I.T. Center for International Studies supported the production and preliminary circulation of this work as a monograph in the Business Management for Economic Development Project series.

TABLE OF CONTENTS

CHAPTER ONE

INTRODUCTION

Reflecting a diversity and complexity of activity, substantial level of financing, and growing levels of external support and internal legitimacy, the proliferation of external non-governmental organizations (NGOs) and indigenous volunteer development organizations (VDOS) [1] has become one of the key, new factors on the African development scene. Partners in activity of the highest priority, the VDOs and the host governments and development finance structures are still evolving the framework of their relationship in Africa.

NGOs (especially Western ones) have a self-image and assessment not only as being among the most effective and efficient providers of development services, but as change agents, mobilizers of local political, organizational and productive resources, often with a tacit, if not explicit, goal of transforming the society and its political system.

Like their less numerous but very significant European counterparts, the American NGOs are becoming very active in Africa, although Central and South America remain their most important arenas. Indeed, the growth of the power, external support, and legitimacy for NGO involvement make them worthy of being understood in their complexity and diversity. Further, it is important to assess the African policy and operational context that is emerging for local and international NGO activity. Some of the major development finance institutions now coming to focus on the issue of NGO/VDO involvement include the World Bank, the African Development Bank, and the host governments.

The NGO/VDO movement merits its rapidly growing significance, considered in terms of the amount of public as well as private money involved. In 1985, the U.S. NGOs channeled nearly $.5 billion worth of service and

---

[1] In many places in this study, we employ the nomenclature decided at the June 1987 meeting of African organizations in Dakar, Senegal. Until then the terms NGO or PVO, from United Nations and other international arenas, was also in widespread use in Africa. We retain these terms in a number of references to industrial country organizations, or in quotes, to reduce confusion.

goods to Africa. In Burkina-Faso alone, in 1986, the NGOs from around the world accounted for about CFA 9.5b (about $29m at mid-1989 $). In Niger, in 1985, VDO activity accounted for about CFA 6.5b.

One should also consider the role they play as nexus between local and global actors, and carriers of new values and skills. Contrary to widely held beliefs, these organizations are not fomenters of revolution or fundamentally destabilizing.[2] Moreover, although their roles are changing and becoming more complex, the tasks they now undertake to promote development and longer term structural change are not new functions; the earlier non-governmental organizations in Europe and North America have always played a significant part in development assistance efforts of the donor governments. They also often have been used to attempt to transfer cultural values and to promote values, social contacts, and political alignments centered and patterned on the donor countries. The NGOs have felt highly uncomfortable with this role and generally belie it in their own public pronouncements and self-image; yet, not just now, but over a fairly long course of time and diverse political and social origins, they have accommodated if not accepted this role.

The truth is that, in the main, whether of the political left or right, whether they say so or not, the NGOs are generally alike, and at home and abroad are often hand-maidens of the governments they presumably seek to change or redirect in the longer run. However, generally, they are considered to be making worthy efforts securing and creating a happier, more secure life for a great many people.

Some of the important characteristics of the NGOs/VDOs in terms of their place in the developmental- and political-change picture, are:

> -- they have an acknowledged record of good performance, in the main, in delivering services and mobilizing people for self help;

> -- the governments do look to the NGOs/VDOs to do what they are sometimes constrained from doing, in both development action and also public education for such action and expenditure, and sometimes for providing cover for the political and social-action agendas of the donor governments;

---

[2] Cf. Brian H. Smith (Ripon College). *Beyond Altruism: The Politics of Private Foreign Aid*. Unpublished. (To be published by Princeton University Press, estimated for 1989.)

-- the NGOs have been able to chart their own course in matters of central principle and to stick to their guns, particularly in Latin America and Eritrea;

-- there is a contrast between their manifest objectives of development promotion and disaster relief and their latent objectives of fundamental social and political change. While it is important in itself, and not a new insight to note this, it is important to highlight the power of the manifest ones, which allow for he preservation of the nexus between the various actors. They honor the manifest ones enough, and these connect powerfully to public values.

The historical record of the Western NGOs also illuminates the basis for some of the American society's dilemma, which demonstrates a deep reservoir of public sentiment and sympathy to help poor people and societies respond to crisis, adjust to or recover from disaster, but not to sustain longer term assistance that seeks lasting structural changes.   The roots of such action were in the post-war relief effort in behalf of European populations, where there were ethnic ties to powerful "majority population" groups in the U.S. The more significant NGOs have carried over to the "Third and Fourth Worlds" much of the formal and manifest goals of the former relief and recovery orientation, but to places that lack equally powerful allied domestic constituencies in the United States. This did and does make it difficult for the U.S. and others successfully to wage the "cold-war".

So, in the public credo and debate, both governments and NGOs have to continue to stress the short-term relief functions, which leave intact perceptions of Third World peoples as marginal and pitiful, rather than the longer term development aspects which would promote their emergence into real actor status in the world, something which the public ethic of U.S. society at large, at least, is not ready for, but the VDOs supposedly are.

One should note the disparate characteristics of the donor country NGOs, especially the sharp differentiation between the U.S. and the rest. Although the "leftist" character of these groups in Canada and Europe may make them vulnerable to political and public pressures in the future, it is an important indication of the character of the general political situation of these countries that their governments do aid and protect these organizations.

There is also a diversity among the types, activities, and orientations of the "less-developed country" (LDC)-based VDOs.   It is also important that despite the generally less widely ranging rhetoric, where the LDC VDOs tend to emphasize achieving fundamental change in favor of common folk, their general political impact in the LDCs is actually rather stabilizing.

In the present study, we cannot explore all the ramifications for recipient African societies of VDO contribution and potential. Whether this new factor of increased VDO involvement, especially from abroad, will enhance the maturation of the development process in Africa or disguise its continued crisis may depend on the policies and processes currently being elaborated at all levels. A number of questions need to be addressed in evaluating the prospects of VDO contributions to African development:

1. Who/what are the relevant actors and what do they do?
2. Do the VDOs and host institutions have common terms
   of reference for their activity?
3. What are the communication problems between the actors?
4. Is there a basic shift occurring in patterns of external
   development-finance assistance?
5. What are the future imperatives that derive from the facts
   and trends regarding VDO activity in Africa?

CHAPTER TWO

**THE RECENT EVOLUTION OF INDIGENOUS AFRICAN NGOS/VDOS
-- LANDMARK MEETINGS --**

I. Introduction:

"The road to Dakar has been long," said the Secretary of the African
NGO Steering Committee in his statement at the opening ceremony of the
historic "First African NGO Conference" [3] held in Dakar, Senegal, 26 May
to 6 June, 1987. "The long road began," he said, "with the struggle for independence by African people and the African NGO meeting marked an
important landmark in the search for a way out of Africa's Economic and
social crisis." [4]

A brief look at certain landmark meetings which preceded the formation
of the Forum of African Volunteer Development Organizations (FAVDO)
provides a useful background on the evolution of change in relationships
between Northern and Southern NGOs which evolved toward the formation
of the coalition of African NGOs represented by the meeting in Dakar in
May 1987.

II. UN Non-Governmental Liaison Service Meetings
(NGLS/Geneva) November 1985

A. Brief Summary

In November of 1985, a meeting entitled: "NGO'S and Africa: A Strategy
Workshop" was organized by the UN NonGovernmental Liaison Service

---

[3] It was the first African conference of such organizations that was
genuinely of continental scope.

[4] Paul Wangoola, "Statement at the Opening Ceremony of the African
NGOs Conference, Dakar, Senegal, 26-28 May, 1987", p. 1.

(NGLS/Geneva).[5] The idea for this workshop emerged from expression of concern over the treatment of the African drought and famine emergency in the media. Both the depiction of the African continent as pathetic and of African people as practically without hope, as well as lack of focus on the history of the crises, led leaders in the Northern and international NGO communities to call for a meeting: "... to bring representatives from Western Europe, North America, Australia, New Zealand and Japan together with their African counterparts to work out cooperative strategies for the next phase of reconstruction, consolidation and long-term development in Africa".)[6]

More than 100 people attended the meeting -- 36 from multilateral agencies and 60 from national and international NGOs, of which only seven were African NGOs. Despite their small numbers, African NGO representatives were influential in the meeting and they worked closely with other participants to develop practical and detailed recommendations to achieve better communications between Northern and Southern NGOs and partnership support for expanding infrastructures of indigenous NGO networks in Africa.

B. Major Issues: Changing Relationships between Northern and Southern
   NGOs

1. Public Education/Advocacy Role for NGOs in the North

At the landmark meetings, certain issues surfaced related to changes in relationships/roles between Northern and Southern NGOs. At the Geneva meeting in November 1985, role distinctions were discussed. Southern NGOs stated that Third World development is their responsibility and they welcome Northern NGO collaboration, not initiative, in the process. They have called on Northern NGOs to expand their home activities in public education and advocacy to promote development. Discussion at the Geneva meeting included Northern and Southern NGO exchange of information in this area. One Northern representative suggested using the public information

---

[5] The workshop was co-sponsored by the United Nations Division for Economic and Social Information (DESTI), the International Coalition for Development Action (ICDA) and the International Council of Voluntary Agencies (ICVA).

[6] "Final Report, NGOs and Africa: A Strategy Workshop." NGLS, Geneva, November, 1985. p iii.

process involved in fund-raising to inform, advocate, change prejudices, and dispel misinformation in their own countries.[7]

Another representative noted that if Northern NGOs come to recognize their role as messengers, rather than providers, they can review their message from a new perspective, and they may find that they have been projecting in their own countries an image of Africans as passive, helpless and pathetic with the belief that Northern NGOs offer cures for these problems. The representative noted that he hoped that instead, the Northern NGO message was a projection of Africans as resilient, capable human beings with enormous endurance and ingenuity. [8]

An example of recommendations from the meeting is the following from a Working Group on Development Education and Campaigning which "...concluded that future development education strategy should: aim to maintain public interest in Africa to emphasize the prevention of future famine, along with food security and the links between the well-being of people in the North and people in the South....change Northern stereotypes of the South...keep Africa in the forefront of public attention in the North."[9]

2. Expanded Support for Indigenous NGOs in the South

Partnership support for expanding infrastructures of indigenous VDO networks in the South and especially in Africa was provided at the Geneva meeting by the following recommendations:

> -- establish a Common Fund for publication and information activities in the South;
> -- reduce the number of development projects and provide more funds for information and communication activities in the South;
> -- improve North/South communications channels;
> -- support the establishment of national and regional coalitions of African NGOs. [10]

---

[7] Final Report, *op.cit.* p. 53.

[8] *Ibid.* p. 53.

[9] Final Report, *op.cit.* 59.

[10] Final Report, *op. cit.* pp. 63-66.

In terms of movement toward equity in relationships between Northern and Southern NGOs and in support for indigenous NGO development, the NGLS/Geneva meeting in November 1985 was a significant landmark.

III. Development Assistance Committee (DAC) Meeting, November 1985

A. Brief Summary

Also meeting in November 1985, the Development Assistance Committee prepared for a DAC Seminar entitled, "The Role of NGOs in Agriculture and Rural Development in Sub-Saharan Africa", which was scheduled for 3-4 June, 1986. [11] The composition of the DAC Committee resulted in the likely exclusion of African NGOs from the proposed seminar, since only NGOs of DAC member countries would automatically be invited to participate. Some representatives in the meeting suggested inviting representatives of African NGOs on the grounds that it would be difficult to discuss issues involving them without their participation. Others, however, were of the opinion that such invitations would be inappropriate at an early stage of the dialogue between DAC members' governments and NGOs. There were some African participants at the June 1986 Seminar.[12]

It should also be noted that at the May/June 1986 NGO meeting associated with the Special Session of the U.N. General Assembly, a Declaration was adopted by representatives of African, Northern, and other international NGOs, that concerned this issue. The meeting endorsed the position presented by the African NGO delegates stating that "Africans are primarily responsible for their own development," with an essential role for African NGOs, while the principal roles for Northern NGOs are to provide support, and seek change in Northern economic and development policies. [13]

---

[11] 495th Meeting, 21 Nov. 1985 at Chateau de la Muette, Paris.

[12] In Chapter IV we report on the participation of Madame Rokiatou Tall, Executive Secretary of the Senegal based AFOTEC.

[13] "The Declaration of Non-Governmental Organisations on The African Economic and Social Crisis". Proceedings of a meeting of African, Northern and International NGOs at the U.N. General Assembly Special Session on the Critical Economic and Social Situation in Africa. 26-32 May 1986.

Despite the outcome, the foregoing illustrates why African VDO representatives have identified the "structure of relationships" with Northern NGOs and international organizations as a source of concern, since African NGOs have been considered "outsiders" who might or might not be invited to meetings addressing issues, and programs involving them. In order to work with other NGOs as collaborators, not recipients, a major objective of African VDOs has been to take initiative and make decisions themselves or with groups of their own choosing.

B. Major Issues: African Voluntary Self-Help Action

African NGO representatives note that the reality of African initiative often goes unnoticed by Northern NGOs who are unaware of or do not focus on African self-help action. This point was raised at an international meeting of NGOs:

"There were several very obvious contradictions involved, for instance between the project activities of NGOs in the field, and the dignity and abilities of the indigenous people. European NGOs had a tendency to explain their activities as if they had sole responsibility for the work of development, and this was a very dangerous impression to project to the public." [14]

1. Recounting the History of African Voluntary Self-HelpAction

African participants at the NGLS meeting pointed out the fact is that African self-help projects abound throughout the continent:

"Most African NGOs which worked at grassroots level were coalitions whose numbers could be anything from two to several hundreds. Some of them, for instance, consisted of groups of two women who had combined their efforts to rear chickens, and sell the eggs to raise the money for school fees for their children. It was small coalitions such as this which had amalgamated to form the large national NGOs who were performing vital development work ... NGOs, particularly in rural areas, were very effective in carrying out their objectives, but their full potential had not been achieved. One reason for this was that whereas many NGOs were groups and affiliations organized by the people themselves to respond to their own needs, the key NGOs had come together as a response to problems, such as those in the areas of energy or the environment, which were national, not individual...Most

---

[14] Final Report. *op. cit.* p 37.

African NGOs had developed by chance, and replaced the strong family relationships which had existed in rural areas before large numbers of people, most of them men, had moved into the towns. Some women, left behind in the rural areas and forced to face family crises alone, had formed women's groups to share the burden of such problems as bereavement ... and coalitions and groups had developed out of the need to find solutions to problems such as these." [15]

The history of African self-help activity illustrates that neither African countries nor African VDOs have been simply recipients of Northern NGO largess. They have been and continue to be major actors in their own behalf. Therefore, the so-called assistential model in which there are Northern donors and African recipients is being challenged in the evolution of change in relationships between the two groups.

2. African Voluntary Self-Help Action: Defining Themselves

Participants also noted that African VDOs have in recent years been establishing lines of communication between individual indigenous VDOs and between national and regional coalitions. This African VDO networking illustrates yet another aspect of change in North/South relationships since formerly Northern NGOs attempted to define what an NGO was or was not. According to their definition, many African self-help groups did not "fit":

"The term 'NGO' was really a misnomer in the context of Africa, when many of them were traditional, village-based associations which frequently had no official status. Strengthening the capacity of these locally-based NGOs, however, posed problems in terms of relation-ships with Northern donors, as most funding was given to projects. This posed serious difficulties for African NGOs. Participatory development projects involved a number of expenses which would not fit under the heading of project costs." [16]

When in March 1986 an "African NGO Steering Committee" was formed, it defined African NGOs on its own terms.
"...an African NGO is one:
(i)   which has arisen in response to the need of the African peoples.
(ii)   whose policy-making organs fully consist of Africans,

---

[15] Final Report, *op. cit.* pp. 14-15.

[16] Final Report, *op.cit.* p. 37.

(iii) where senior staff whose decisions are likely to influence policy
       are also African,

(iv)   and NGOs which have a constituency and a framework for
       democratic participation and account ability."[17]

3. African Voluntary Self-Help Action: Initiating A
    Continental Organization

The evolution of the development of the African NGO Steering Commit-
tee was closely related to events surrounding the UN Special Session on
Africa held in May, 1986. Describing the establishment of the Steering
Committee, Secretary Paul Wangoola stated at the Dakar African NGO
Forum meeting in May 1987:

"As members of the NGO community, we are happy that African
Governments, Northern Governments, and International development
agencies recognized the importance of NGO participation in resolving
the Economic and Social crisis which afflicts Africa, to the extent they
accepted NGOs to provide inputs on the diagnosis of and prescription
for the African crises, and to participate in the UN Special Session on
Africa. And within the global community of NGOs, it is significant to
note that they easily and quickly agreed that the African NGOs should
give the lead in the preparation of NGOs' views on the African crisis,
its nature and origins; as well as suggestions and proposals on ways out
of this crisis....It was in pursuance of this mandate that an African
NGO Steering Committee was set up during March 1986; and was
convened in Nairobi during April 1986. In Nairobi, the African NGOs
Steering Committee prepared a Position Paper on the Economic and
Social Crisis in Africa; as well as made proposals on possible ways out
of this crisis. The African NGOs attending the Special Session of the
UN decided to establish an African NGO Forum...to provide a
framework for information flow and exchange, mutual support, joint
actions, and a framework for strengthening communication channels
with Governments." [18]

The first meeting of the African NGO Forum (later named FAVDO)
was in Dakar in May 1987. Before discussing that meeting, we assess the
other important landmark meetings held since the Special Session of the
U.N. General Assembly.

---

[17] Paul Wangoola, Statement, Opening Ceremony, *op.cit.* p. 7.

[18] *Ibid*. p. 4-5.

IV. Overseas Development Institute and the Journal
of World Development Meeting, London, March 1987

A. Brief Summary

In April of 1987, several months earlier than the Dakar meeting that created the FAVDO, another landmark meeting was held when more than 100 development professionals from 42 countries met in London for a Symposium co-sponsored by the Overseas Development Institute and the journal *World Development* on "Development Alternatives: The Challenge for NGOs". Representatives to that meeting came from 28 "developing" and 14 "developed" countries and much of the discussion focused on North/South relationships including statements: "...calling for a genuine *partnership* between northern and southern NGOs to replace previous dependence, mistrust and paternalism." [19]

B. Major Issue: Change in Relationships between Northern and Southern
   NGOs

African NGOs' concern with the "structure" of the relationships in which initiative and decisions are made by Northern NGOs was echoed by other Southern NGO representatives. At this meeting, a suggested Code of Conduct, providing guidelines for North/South relationships, received considerable support. A particular focus in the discussion was the question of resources for NGOs - including resources other than funds. Informational exchange was considered a crucial resource as well as the improvement of the technical and organizational capacities of human resources.

Problems of funding centered on the Southern NGOs argument that core funding rather than project funding encourages capacity-building and long-term planning. Project-funding was seen as encouraging a piecemeal approach to development activities. The meeting also included discussion of evaluation effectiveness, research priorities, networking, development education and advocacy and NGO relations with Governments. The meeting was particularly significant because it represented movement in the direction of a more collaborative model in North/South NGO relationships and movement away from the assistential model. The direction of movement is important at this period of increasing worldwide emphasis on development

---

[19] Preliminary Report, "Development Alternatives: The Challenge for NGOs," Overseas Development Institute, London, March, 1987, p. 3.

assistance through NGOs. NGOs are viewed as promoters of alternative development strategies. Therefore, changes in internal relationships between Northern and Southern NGOs representing greater collaboration, rather than paternalism, will serve to strengthen NGO development strategies. The meeting report noted:

"A corollary to this is the fundamental shift from the northern NGOs to the Southern NGOs as the leaders of the development process in the Third World. Southern NGOs strongly emphasized that development in the Third world is their responsibility -- from setting the development priorities to implementing projects to generating more of their own funds." [20]

V. South/South NGO Meeting in London

A. Brief Summary

In order to discuss their own priorities, NGO representatives from Southern NGOs stayed in London two additional days following the Symposium. This South-South Cooperation Conference took note of the historical context in which people of the Third World strive to improve their lives through self-reliance and indicated their support for that struggle through two essential steps:

1) renegotiation of the principles and terms of North/South interaction to achieve equity in those relationships; and 2) strengthening South-South cooperation to encourage great-er sharing of resources and experiences.

B. Major Concern: Strengthening South/South Cooperation

Participants emphasized the need to exchange/use Southern experience and expertise in the fields of community mobilization, credit union management, environmental issues, technology and other areas such as the experience of women in development. They pointed out that Northern women's liberation movements don't reflect the issues of Southern -- particularly rural -- women. "Women in the South," notes the Report, "have to bear the brunt of the fragile economies and the concomitant trade pricing related

---

[20] Preliminary Report, "Development Alternatives: The Challenge for NGOs," Overseas Development Institute, London, March, 1987, p. 2.

shocks especially in Africa." [21] They called for sharing of Southern experiences and related studies on the survival and self-reliance of women's groups on different continents.

NGO representatives reporting at the FAVDO conference on the South--South meeting held in London said that rather than establish a permanent structure at the meeting, representatives decided to get feedback from each of their country NGO organizations to determine how the South-South network should establish itself and they should convene another event to distill that information and move South- South cooperation forward.

At the FAVDO Conference a team of African delegates met with other Southern delegates to work out proposals for exchange in areas considered must urgent: information and personnel. To facilitate such exchange, it was proposed that documentation centers be identified for each region represented. Centers were identified in Dakar, Senegal; Manila, The Philippines; New Delhi, India; and Dominica, The West Indies. The agencies designated in each place were selected as temporary Documentation Centers, but ongoing contact agencies. Further South-South activities are to be determined by FAVDO's consultation with other Southern Regions.

VI. The Enabling Environment Conference. Nairobi, October 1986

A. Brief Summary

The Enabling Environment Conference to promote Effective Private Sector Contribution to Development in Sub-Saharan Africa was held in Nairobi, Kenya, 21-24 October, 1986. The primary objective of the Conference was to facilitate dialogue resulting in a range of practical policy options that would enable the private sector to operate more positively in the development process in Africa.

More than 200 representatives of governments, private development agencies (PDAs) and private business from over 25 African, European and North American nations attended the Conference. Over two-thirds of the participants were African, and needs and priorities of the Continent were openly discussed in frank debate with varying points of view. The broad themes of discussion were the relationship between African governments and

---

[21] A Report on the Proceedings of the South-South Non-Governmental Development Organization Cooperation Conference, London, 14-15 March, 1987. p. 10.

private business and/or PDAs and the promotion of dialogue among the three sectors based on the concept of "social responsibility".

B. Conference Recommendations

Conference discussion regarding the work and promise of PDAs is especially relevant within the framework of the evolution of FAVDO because of their importance as examples of voluntary, self-help, non-profit, participatory organizations which promote cost-effective development. A specific request of the Conference was that national councils of PDAs be strengthened and that they develop mutually supportive relationships with international PDAs. The recent creation of FAVDO represents a movement in that direction.

Conference participants also urged PDAs to develop closer relationships with business and government in order to strengthen their voluntary efforts through improved management, training and financial support. This is an issue that was taken up at the subsequent FAVDO meeting.

VII. Forum of African Voluntary Development Organizations --   FAVDO Meeting. Dakar, May-June 1987.

A. Brief Summary

The first continent-wide meeting of African NGOs in Dakar, Senegal, 26 May-5 June, 1987, brought together 71 delegates from 23 African countries representing indigenous voluntary organizations from Francophone, Anglophone, Lusophone, and Arabic-speaking Africa. Joining them were 67 representatives of NGOs from Asia, Latin America, Europe, and North America, as well as African Governments, and officials of International non-governmental organizations and donor agencies.

Conference objectives presented at the meeting stressed not only collaboration among African NGOs and a new understanding and framework for North/South cooperation, but also the objective of establishing dialogue with African Governments, "...in order to secure official recognition for NGOs and as a means towards NGO participation and partnership in development." [22] Throughout their development, networks of African NGOs have stressed the need for close association with their governments. At the Conference, there were two sessions for meetings with African governments,

---

[22] FAVDO,"(Preliminary) Proceedings of the African NGO Conference." Dakar, Senegal, 26 May - 5 June 1987 p. 5.

one in which African NGOs met to discuss methods for effective partnership in development, and a second session in which Southern, Northern and international NGOs were invited to join their African counterparts in meeting with African Government representatives to discuss the more general role of NGOs as partners with government in development.

B. FAVDO Conference Outcomes

1. A very significant outcome of the Conference is that it provided African VDO representatives an opportunity to meet each other, learn about voluntary development programs throughout the continent, exchange ideas, and formulate ideas for further networking, exchange and cooperation. This is an extremely important outcome because volunteers are often forced to work in isolation and they frequently cite the need for contact and information about others' experiences in similar development efforts. In sum, as actors in voluntary development efforts, the African VDO representatives viewed the Conference and the Forum as opportunities to learn how to improve their development activities. The Conference was, therefore, constantly filled with the vitality of people eager to talk to and learn from each other.

2. A corollary to the importance of meeting and exchanging ideas and experiences is the importance of discussing agenda/priorities/concerns defined by the African NGOs themselves. In contrast, the common experience for representatives of African NGOs invited to meetings convened by Northern/International NGOs is that they are invited to make input into an agenda which had been previously defined by, or through sheer numbers will be dominated by, representatives of those Northern/International NGOs. Thus, the formation of an African chorus including voices from a wide range of voluntary organizations throughout the continent gives African NGO's powerful representation in meetings where they were formerly represented in isolated, usually small, numbers. Much time was, therefore, spent in making their voices heard. The FAVDO Conference proceedings then can be seen as a statement of solidarity and collaboration as well as self-definition, self-direction and self-reliance.

The change of terms from "NGO" to "VDO" is important to note in the context of self-definition.   There was considerable discussion between Africans and with Northerners and other Southerners about the use of the word "voluntary" rather than "private". Near the end of the meeting, "...it was agreed that the introduction of the term "Voluntary" (in VDO) was a desirable development; it is the sense of volunteerism that matters -- the spirit of freedom to participate -- without compulsion." [23]   It is also a matter of freedom to define oneself as one chooses -- without compulsion -- that is illustrated in the change in terms.

3.   Formal establishment of the African NGO Forum was a major outcome of the meeting.   This Pan African Forum of African Voluntary Organizations (FAVDO) has a Governing Council and a Technical (Advisory) Task Force which produced a preliminary draft Constitution adopted in spirit by the Forum.

4. Of particular significance was the opportunity the FAVDO Conference afforded for continuation of the South/South solidarity meeting which began in London in March following the International NGO meeting entitled "Development Alternatives: The Challenge for NGOs".   Following that meeting, representatives from Southern NGOs met for two days to discuss common issues and concerns and formulate strategies for continued collaboration.   At the Dakar meeting, representatives from Latin America and Asia joined African NGO reps to discuss key areas for South/South cooperation which were identified as 1) self-reliance, 2) communication and 3) resource exchanges.   Particular focus for informational exchange will be put on: water development, soil conservation, health, women and development and traditional medicine.

5.   A very important outcome of the FAVDO conference was the opportunity it provided for continued discussion of the changes occurring in North/South NGO relationships related to the change from a "donor-recipient" to a " collaborative" model.   This structural change in relationships requires change in: a) decision-making, b) funding, c) accountability, d) reporting and e) evaluation.

a. Decision-Making

In the context of discussions about movement from aid to solidarity, there was agreement that the new North/South partnership relations call for partnership decision-making with great increase in the information available to the South from the North about the political dynamics, the fund-raising process and amounts and policy activities in which Northern NGOs are involved in their own countries.

---

[23] FAVDO (Preliminary) Proceedings, *op.cit.*, p. 42.

b. Funding

There is general agreement about the need for direct funding from Northern to Southern NGOs (for institution-building as well as projects) and anticipation that Southern NGOs must prepare to handle both the rise in direct funding and possible political interference while North/South partnerships should establish alternative funding structures to handle Northern Government funds. In order to achieve greater North/South NGO partnership, and more Southern control where Northern NGOs depend on Governments, the following recommendations were made:
  -- National counterparts of Northern NGOs should control a portion of resources through agreed-upon national mechanisms;
  -- Northern NGOs will co-finance actions of Southern National Groups
  -- FAVDO should identify countries and coordinating agencies in a pilot country;
  -- FAVDO should compile guidelines for funding and consult with NGOs.

With regard to various forms of funding, such as grants and loans, there was a recommendation that African VDOs should jointly decide with grassroots communities, the framework and types of funding to be used. There was also a recommendation that African VDOs should first mobilize resources available within Africa, and when Northern NGOs are called upon to participate, it should be on a matching basis in the form of grants until Southern VDOs become financially autonomous.

The possibility of enhancing relationships between VDOs and businesses was discussed at the FAVDO meeting, including requests to the business sector for assistance through contributions to an Endowment Fund:

"It was suggested that all commercial ventures operating in African countries should be requested to pay 2½% of their profits to fund VDOs or recognized development projects, and that payment should be tax deductible." Requests to governments were not for financial assistance but: "...for such enabling facilities as exemption from customs duty and taxes on materials connected with the development functions of NGOs." [24]

c. Accountability

Having accepted that the grassroots is the group to which both Northern and Southern NGOs must be accountable, there was general agreement that

---

[24] *Ibid.*

recommendations regarding relationships with this group should be included in a Code of Conduct governing North/South relations.   More specific recommendations called for greater grassroots involvement in program development, implementation, evaluation and management and greater openness from Northern and Southern NGOs regarding funds, other resources and conditionalities.

d. Reporting

In addition to recommending greater interaction with the grassroots at all stages of program implementation so that reporting would be part of the enhanced process of accountability, the group also recommended that the proposed Code of Conduct "assure exposure at local and international levels of unprincipled behaviors by NGOs of North and South." [25]

e. Evaluation

It was recommended that grassroots persons be involved in co-evaluation of programs of development.

6. Discussion with donor agencies regarding approaches to development, funding priorities, and requirements and specific strategies for addressing the current African crises, was a significant outcome of the FAVDO meeting since it represented the first opportunity these agencies had to listen to the ideas, concerns, and suggestions of African NGO representatives from throughout the continent regarding their view of donor agencies activities in Africa. It was a unique opportunity for feedback.

7. The FAVDO Conference provided a very visible stage upon which African NGOs could present their position regarding their relationship to African governments. During their preparatory meeting at the UN Special Session on Africa, African NGO representatives noted in their Summary Record some primary expectations:

"(vii) Explain to African Governments that African NGOs are partners and not competitors in development.

---

[25] *Ibid.*, p. 33.

(viii) Sensitize Governments on the need for institutionalizedchannels of communications with NGOs."[26]

Similarly, in Document 2A, a background document presented at the Dakar Conference as incorporating an initial framework for the creation of an African NGO Forum, the planners state:

"This conference will provide a suitable opportunity for African NGOs to re-affirm their faith in, and recognition of Governments as our major partners in development in Africa, understanding that they have the political responsibility for social and economic development of the people; to seek cooperation with African Governments on the role NGOs must play: to discuss areas and methodologies for effective partnership in development." [27]

Finally, at the FAVDO meeting in which African NGOs met with representatives from African governments, the FAVDO Secretary-General "...identified the FAVDO position on a number of issues which were central to an understanding of its role and functions, and its relationship with Governments." He stated that African VDOs recognize that:

(i) African Governments have political responsibility.
(ii) African Governments have prime responsibility for development.
(iii) VDOs have no political ambitions.
(iv) As far as development is concerned, African VDOs have responsibility, in consultations with grassroots, whose needs we propose to address; Northern NGOs can only play a supporting role.
(v) As VDOs, the African NGOs have access to resources which are not normally available to Governments.
(vi) African Governments, collectively and individually must dialogue with Northern Governments." [28]

These comments reflected very broad concern among the FAVDO participants with improving relationships with their governments. This was

---

[26] "Summary Record of the Preparatory Meeting of African Delegates to the UN General Assembly Special Session on the African Crisis, May 25, 1986," p. 2.

[27] FAVDO Conference, Document 2-A, p. 17.

[28] FAVDO (Preliminary) Proceedings. *op.cit.*, p. 40.

a major part of the discussions and the following recommendation was adopted in the final resolution: "In order to eliminate misunderstanding, African NGOs should initiate better channels of communication and continuing dialogue with the Governments." [29]

All of the statements above are designed to assure African Governments of African NGOs' desire for approval, formal recognition and serious consideration as collaborators in development. While there are indications that many African Governments take seriously the NGO phenomenon as an aspect of development, it is not yet clear that they view indigenous African NGOs as collaborators in developing national policy or strategies or in making Africa's general interests and concerns understood in meetings of international NGOs and multilateral donor agencies.

VIII. FAVDO Follow-up Meeting. Nairobi, July 1987.

A. Brief Summary

The Governing Council of FAVDO held its first post inaugural meeting in Nairobi between 23-31 July, 1987 when Council members were guests at the meeting of the AALAE, the African Association of Literacy and Adult Education, a specialized network of educational workers and organizations. FAVDO has adopted the strategy of supporting AALAE and similar networks created by African NGOs specializing in the fields of: environment, women and development, research and training, health and integrated rural development. FAVDO will serve as a facilitating agency for networks of African NGOs to:
-- identify the most effective strategies to mobilize available human, material, and financial resources within and outside the continent;
-- determine the most effective use of resources; and
-- provide a platform for coordination, cooperation, collaboration and mutual support among African NGOs.

B. Major Actions

1. In order to identify the expertise, resource base, institutional capacity, capability and needs of African NGOs, the Council has initiated action on an African NGO Directory and a Needs-Assessment Survey.

---

[29] *loc. cit.*

2. To develop an operational strategy and budget for the policy of network support, the Council commissioned a Programming Conference and Training Workshop for November 1987.

3. In its discussion of the critical Southern African situation, the Council noted with satisfaction and expressed its solidary with the struggle of many indigenous voluntary organizations working to uphold and maintain the dignity of the oppressed people of South Africa. Noting with concern the escalation of tension, repression, and destabilization in Southern Africa, FAVDO is exploring, in consultation with voluntary development organizations in Southern and South Africa, "...the possibilities of an African People's Conference on Southern Africa to identify new strategies to accelerate the process of a peaceful and democratic change within the shortest possible time to avert the creation of a holocaust in Southern Africa." [30]

4. The Council also expressed concern regarding "...the hostile international, financial, political and military environment within which the peoples of the Third World, especially Africa, have to struggle for the survival of their ecological environment, culture and ways of life." [31] To address this concern, FAVDO will try to assemble a South-South Commission of eminent third-world persons to prepare a 'Plan of Action for Survival.'

5. At the conclusion of its meeting, "... the Council reiterated FAVDO's commitment to address itself to issues related to African development in forms that are culturally acceptable, environmentally sound, self-reliant, sustainable, and participatory." [32]

IX. Northern NGO/International Organizations Meeting in Response to FAVDO. New York, June 1987.

A. Brief Summary:

An informal meeting of Northern NGOs and International Organizations was held in New York in late June to "consider the Dakar Conference and information-sharing among indigenous African NGOs." The need for reorienting their relationships with African VDOs appeared to be acknowledged by the group, when, following some early discussion of leadership

---

[30] FAVDO Communique 1 August 87, p. 3.

[31] *Loc. cit.*

[32] *Loc. cit.*

development within FAVDO and its exclusion of African VDOs that are a division of Northern NGOs or which have over-representation of Northerners on their Boards, meeting attendants observed that there was firm adherence to these views within FAVDO because African VDOs want assurance that each member's policy is *controlled by Africans* In short, decisions about internal leadership and membership could be discussed by, but not controlled by non-Africans.

B. Suggested Northern NGO Meeting Topics:

Acknowledgement of what was termed: " ...a new way of doing business" propelled the discussion toward suggestions regarding proposed meetings of Northern NGOs to consider topics such as:

1) change in North/South relationships and reorienting Northern
   policy toward African NGOs;
2) how to support African NGOs;
3) amount of resources being invested in strengthening African NGOs
   and how to effect such strengthening;
4) making greater use of African consultants and researchers;
5) managing Northern demands on African NGOs for project data.

C. Modes of Supporting FAVDO: Present and Future

Discussion indicated that Canadian initiatives have demonstrated the greatest support for African NGOs. PAC has firmly refused support for any Canadian NGO projects which don't strengthen African NGOs. Anticipating PAC's support for FAVDO, one attendant noted PAC's efforts to get other Canadian institutions and municipalities to strengthen African organizations.

US initiatives demonstrating support of African NGOs include a PACT project funding management training in collaboration with the Malian NGO umbrella organization, CCA, and an Industry Council for Development (ICD) project linking business corporations with indigenous NGOs.

Attenders anticipated strengthening of FAVDO at the international level, since it may obtain Observer Status at the OAU. The group also noted that African leaders "struck a note of self-reliance" similar to the message from Dakar at their recent meeting reviewing progress in implementing recommendations from the UN Special Session on Africa; and there will be a new staff person, responsible for NGO relations, within the new Secretariat established by the UN Secretary-General to oversee the implementation of the African recovery program.

NGLS/Geneva is planning a conference in February 1988 on Africa's recovery from the famine emergency and the representative stressed the importance of involving Africans in planning and carrying out that meeting. It is, therefore, highly unlikely that the meeting will be like a similar meeting in 1985 which had a low level of African input although the topic under discussion was the African crises. It is quite likely that events of the intervening two years in which African VDOs have established their continental organization will greatly influence the dynamics and outcomes of the upcoming NGLS/Geneva meeting.

The informal meeting of Northern NGOs and International Organizations concluded with emphasis on the importance of supporting FAVDO and requests for new modes and models in North-South cooperation.

CHAPTER THREE:

SELECTED CASE STUDIES OF WEST AFRICAN COUNTRIES: PERCEPTIONS BY VDO AND GOVERNMENT LEADERS REGARDING PEOPLE/PRODUCT/PLACE/PROCEDURES/PROBLEMS/PROSPECTS OF VDOS IN DEVELOPMENT

CASE ONE -- NIGER

I. Introduction

Niger provides what is, perhaps, the real test case for external VDOs in the Western Sahel region of Africa. It is regarded by many leaders in the VDO community as involving the most demanding and rigid frameworks within which they have to work in West Africa. It is there also that one finds the most coherent and formalized governmental philosophy of grass-roots based development action, in an effort to reconstruct society into a "Société de Développement" directed by "initiatives de base." It is an effort to "développer a la base, étape par étape" -- a step-by-step development effort from the bottom up.

Wrapped in the rhetorical splendor of the late President Kountche's vision, the effort proclaims its aim to be to "résponsibiliser la paisannérie", to put the peasant in charge. It remains to be seen if this vision will outlive its author, or if it can even begin to capture and transform reality. If not, the peasants, and those that attempt to work most directly with and for them, may find themselves more mired than ever in layers of bureaucratic miasma. Niger is a hot and remote, low key and slow moving, proud and politically experienced country, one that is among the hardest hit by drought and poverty. The external VDO leadership confronts officials whom they describe as being inscrutable and as demanding as officials anywhere are, of exact compliance with very elaborate registration, planning, and operational procedures. Much as the country may need money, it does not stoop to find it, and, with little dryness of throat, said goodbye to Bob Geldof and his Live Aid/Band Aid Organization, when the latter said they couldn't satisfy such regulations. On first view, the place looks forbidding. Yet, a great many of the larger and more experienced international VDOs are happily at work here, and their actual experience suggests there are fewer reporting requirements than elsewhere, and those who take the trouble to touch the proper bases can accomplish their tasks reasonably quickly.

II. Perceptions by Niger VDO Leaders:

A. VDO Perceptions about the Actors -- People/ Products

1. Indigenous Organizations:

There are few indigenous organizations that are members of the 'Groupement des Aides Privées' (GAP), the federation that officially represents the VDO community. Indeed, we were told there are really only two "real 'NGOs,' strictly speaking" that are indigenous, the "Croix Rouge" and the "Églises évangeliques", both of which are the creations of external organizations. A World Bank study mission to the country in 1982 to assess potential for VDO activity there noted that "the only totally Nigerien groups that could qualify as private voluntary organizations are the traditional "associations villageoises", the formal cooperatives, the 'Samaria' movement and the 'Union des Femmes Nigeriènnes,' (UFN). They all mobilize a large number of people. Not all of their activities are spontaneous but, on the whole, they do marshall a mass of individuals (for) voluntary efforts to practical ends...they are development engines, so to speak, and can direct important, self-motivated human resources toward ... (development) projects." [33]

Definitions may count for a great deal in this situation. The grand brotherhoods among the Muslims are not counted in this community of mostly Christian-inspired and state-registered formal organizations that comprise the VDO "community" in Niger. At the village level, Niger is not different from other West African cases discussed here, in terms of the associations, groups, cooperatives etc. that exist. The GAP does not seek to bring them in as members, perhaps for the same reasons that their sister, but much more localized agency, the SPONG in Burkina Faso, does not; because these indigenous associations are not designed to operate outside a given very local area.

The World Bank mission noted that the Union des Femmes Nigeriènnes (UFN) had received some assistance from Croix Rouge and the Church World Service (CWS) in vegetable garden projects involving improved traditional irrigation techniques, and in a project involving the manufacture and sale (at a highly subsidized price) of improved woodstoves. The UFN

---

[33] World Bank "Office Memorandum" from V. Masoni, IRD, to Mrs. Shirley Boskey, Director, IRD., 7 December 1982. p. 1.

gathers the requests for the stoves that were initially manufactured by the CWS, but later this function was taken over by the UFN, with the CWS providing only continuing financial assistance and technical back-stopping.

The Samaria Movement is a traditional Muslim movement among women, who combine the organization of cultural and dance groups with the conduct of development projects such as reforestation. It is cited by the government as one of the best examples of participatory democratic action at the local level. The movement has also received support from the Croix Rouge and the UFN.

2. Expatriate Organizations:

The "Groupement des Aides Privées" (GAP) is essentially an organization of expatriate VDOs. Although open to all, its leadership reflects its over-whelming expartiate membership. Established in 1975, it has operated with a very small staff, and not only serves to bring the VDOs together to share information and experience, but also serves the important function of gathering project proposals that have come into the government, or been elaborated by it, to present to the VDOs for their adoption and implementa-tion. A World Bank mission described the operation as follows:

"it gathers projects suitable for NGO financing and submits them to its members accordingly. The projects are: (a) proposed by the local population; (b) approved by local government authorities (usually the sous-prefet); (c) reviewed by the relevant ministries; and (d) sent to the national GAP Correspondent, an official of the Ministry of Rural Development, who presents the projects to GAP at monthly meetings. Each member has full discretion as to which projects to select for its own involvement. Once an NGO has decided to provide finance/ staff for a project, the NGO and the GAP Correspondent negotiate a project agreement (protocol executif.) ... On the whole, NGOs find the system smooth, although some of them admit that the project portfolio brought to them is more a shopping list than a section of an overall investment program...In the context of an austere regime such as that of Niger, the system may be a realistic compromise bet-ween socio-political realities and the need for economic allocation of resources. While the total NGO contribution to Niger is not at all negligible for so poor a country, a comparison with the NGO inputs in Upper Volta (sic) strongly suggests that the GAP system may be too confining; more funds would likely flow if a more relaxed approach were adopted." [34]

The report also points out that the projects submitted to the GAP usually require two to three years to be implemented, after which the local population is to take them over and the NGO is required to move on to a new area. "This way, no NGO sets up a permanent area of influence," they were told by one of the GAP member organization leaders.

The report also asserted that the Government of Niger (GON) makes no effort to inform NGOs about large-scale development schemes in which they could fit, or of findings that have implications for their operations, and that NGOs need to be exposed to the problems of large-scale development. The mission felt that the Bank should work more closely with NGOs in Niger, as elsewhere.

The GAP's own annual report for 1986 describes its development, interests and accomplishments in the following terms:

"The first role of GAP, which was assigned to it by the small circle of NGOs that were here at the time of the great drought of the 1970s, is precisely to offer a structure which responds to felt needs (of the people). It was a manifestly fortunate initiative because from the small circle, the membership has grown to twenty-two (1985) or about half the NGOs operating in Niger...More than a structure of information exchange and coordination, the GAP is an accepted intermediary between the public authorities and the NGO community, a responsibility which it carries out with strict respect for the autonomy and philosophy of each one of its members.

"In the accomplishment of the tasks which are assigned to it, the GAP is favored by two key factors: the participation of the people at large. On these bases it has organized five seminars (1979 in Agadez, 1981 at Niamey, 1982 at Maradi, 1983 Dosso, and 1984 at Diffa) with the double aim of having the technical administrators and local communities and the NGOs better know each other and become familiar with the structures and the working methods of the NGOs; and at the same time, to permit the latter to listen to the milieu in

---

[34] World Bank , *op.cit.*, pp. 2, 3.

which they work and better know the problems which the   rural world faces daily." [35]

Church World Service was probably the first of the external VDOs to come to Niger in the early 1970s. It is now the second largest development program, emphasizing health projects in the North, riverbank protection projects, including road-building, and education in the Tuareg area of Kari, pilot reforestation projects in Keita district, school gardens and lowland development in Maradi. They were followed by CARE, initially to provide relief supplies and moving on to development projects in 1975. Recently they have been active in agro-forestry, dune stabilization and windbreaks projects, education, and emergency assistance. In 1986 CARE expended nearly 700 million CFA on eight projects. The only larger program that year was the "Association française des voluntaires pour le progrès", the French volunteers program, which expended nearly a billion francs on 46 projects.

Altogether the VDO community has carried out 143 projects in 1986, worth over 4 billion CFA ($13m in mid 1987). This activity was reasonably well spread around the country, with the Diffa and Dosso departments well below the average. These are areas of considerable population, especially Dosso, but ones where there is already some development.

3. Government Institutions:

The GAP leadership has most of its contact with the "Micro-Réalisations" Division of the Ministry of Plan. At the local levels they will also have close contact with the administrative officials for the unit, whether it be arrondissement, départment, etc. in which they work. There was some sentiment expressed that carrying out the contacts with the various governmental agencies to which they must relate can be very time consuming. (See more under the "procedures" section, below.)

B. VDO Perceptions of Issues of Place -- Spacial Location:

This was not raised as a problem by the VDO leadership. Their greater concern was that the projects really come from the people, and reflect their readiness to contribute to their implementation. For this reason, AFRICARE did not join the GAP system for a number of years, preferring, and somehow being allowed, to get projects directly from local groups.

---

[35] GAP. *Organizations Non-Gouvernementales, Niger.* 1986. p. 1.

C. VDO Perceptions about Procedures:

1. Registration/ Authorization:

There are two types of protocol required, according to the VDO leadership:

l) a "protocol type", the basic framework agreement that authorizes the organization to operate. It gives very wide scope of activity and includes exoneration from payment of tax and import duty payments.

2) the "protocol de mise en application" that specifically defines the project activities and conditions of the operation, including the specific governmental services and agencies that will be involved, through the "Préfet", such as the "Chef de l'instance", up to the ministries. It is for the VDO to have worked out these terms of the project with regard to the objectives, activities, and financing. However, after all this is done and the protocol agreed upon, it commits both sides.

To receive the initial authorisation to operate, the VDO has to supply several items of information and documentation (with five copies each): a) minutes of the first meeting ever held by the organization; b) minutes of the meeting at which it decided to come to Niger, and c) the organizational charter. With these documents, which allows the government to know the basic objectives and character of the organization, what it wants to do in Niger, the organization goes to the specific technical ministry concerned with the subject of their project(s) to get their approval. Then it must go to the Ministry of Interior to get the general "arrêté" that permits it to operate. After that, one must get an implementation protocol from the Ministry of Plan ("Micro-réalisations" department). The process can be cumbersome and take a long time, say the VDO leaders. An example was given by one of them where the original filing occurred in October, but it wasn't until 2 March that the organization could have personal contact with the appropriate officer, which produced a letter of agreement the very next day, but it wasn't until 10 May that the arre^té came through, permitting them to exist and operate. Then they had to work our the implementation agreements.

The VDOs also complain that the system is cumbersome in operation. For projects in the field, the line of contact has to be, the "Chef d'arrondissement", then the "Sous-Préfet", then the "Préfet", then the technical Ministry involved, then the Ministry of Plan, and that sequence holds for every twist in the implementation of the project. A VDO has to lobby, walk the corridors, to go the rounds and promote itself to get things done.

2. Communication:

GAP leadership asserted that all these requirements and contacts can be carried out in a short period of time. One leader of a major VDO also claimed his organization had absolutely no problem in making the system work, at the local or the national level. Protocol and procedure is very important, as is communication with and courtesy to the administrative officials. But if one does this, there are few hindrances. Indeed, one VDO leader said that after frequent visits to the administrative officials during the start-up phases of projects, so that these officials know who you are and what you are doing, the on-going notification and communication can be done by telephone, despite the fact that the official rules could require each person who makes a visit to the field to inform the local officials at each level at least two weeks in advance.

GAP leadership acknowledges, however, that local leaders, themselves, will get into trouble if the state administrative authority cannot submit a report covering their activities each six months. The integrated rural development projects have to submit reports regularly. One VDO leader felt these procedures might not apply if the organization has "no collaboration with the state, and if the VDO has its own personnel on the ground". The reports submitted are an enumeration of activities, not an evaluation of them. Also, the local structures of the state are there to help elaborate the projects, all of which then have to be presented to the central government in order to descend again to the local level.

3. Tax/ duties/ privileges:

Problems are emerging in this area. The VDOs complain that they are now subject to the Value-Added-TAx which varies between 25% and 35%, and now averages about 27%. They feel that this is too much for the VDOs to pay; it negates their aid, and they note that in Niger, as in almost all other countries, the official bi-lateral aid programs are exempted from this tax.   However, by the terms of their official protocols, the VDOs are obliged to pay it. The GAP is engaging in what might best be termed "collective bargaining" on behalf of the whole of the VDO community to get an exemption from these taxes.

4. Freedom:

The rigorous registration and approval procedures might suggest very rigid and narrow frameworks within which the VDOs must work. In practice, once the organizations are satisfied they have workable and important projects, they are given wide latitude to determine their own level of commitments. They are relatively constrained from going into local areas and finding their own counterpart groups and village alliances.

One mechanism of control over the implementation activity that the government requires is the disbursement of funds to local projects only through accounts in which the local administrators have joint signature. Thus, money cannot be spent locally until both sides agree. Yet, in practice, the VDO leaders have said that they have no experience where the countersignature was withheld.

5. Funding: There were no comments made about funding procedures.

6. Plan Fit: VDO leaders expressed the belief that this would be assured by the procedures of project identification and selection/authorization.

D. VDO Perceptions of Problems:

1. Tax Exemption: See the above discussion of procedures.
2. Government Attention/ Tolerance of VDOs:

The Niger government's interest in promoting VDOs is thought to be somewhat mixed. VDOs point to the lack of any real evaluation process. They claim that government interest depends on whether the individual person involved, Préfet, Sous-Préfet, etc., takes a keen interest. There is no governmental requirement to receive VDO reports or to see the reports they may send to their affiliates abroad. There have been no government requests to the VDOs for reports, and some groups claimed never to have sent in one.

E. VDO Perceptions of Prospects

Funding: One group felt that there would be some funding available to local groups through the GAP, but that organization's leadership did not mention this possibility.

III. Perceptions by Niger Government/International Organizations

A. Government Perceptions about the Actors -- People/Product:

1. Indigenous Organizations:

The Niger government officials we interviewed named only the Croix Rouge, the Union des Femmes Nigeriènnes, the Conseil des églises évangeliques, and the Samaria as examples of indigenous groups. This list accords with that given by the VDO leaders themselves. These government officials asserted that the GAP is the appropriate focal point for any study of the VDOs.

They regret that there is not yet an organization among the university students and graduates to undertake VDO action. "Ils n'ont pas la notion de service à la nation" argued one high official. However, he did also say that school leavers and university students are often called upon (successfully, one presumes) to come to the aid of the village groups and cooperatives.

The government continues to promote cooperatives and the mutual aid organizations, "Grouppements de mutualité" (GM), at the village level, and the Unions rurales communautaires (URC) at the level of Sous-Prefets, but feels that most of these are not really functional, and are not playing their proper role. Niger envisions a cooperative formation for the general society and wants each cooperative project to have a trained staff person capable of good management. Usually, however, the General Manager of the cooperatives, which is likely to be the one cadre these groups may have, is not paid but, rather, receives goods in kind from the people. In such groups, the government attempts to conduct basic literacy training in the villages, using simple ideogram systems, and is trying to teach basic accounting and organizational skills, so that the group itself can note the production achieved, and to provide a VDO-like framework for local action. The "Samarias" were praised as a good example of the desired type of local participatory, democratic organizations in action.

However, the government believes that none of these local groups is really able to be self-financing. One official argued that with even high governmental functionaries receiving a salary that amounts to about $550 a month, one could not expect the people lower in the scale to have enough money to do something valuable for themselves, and for the community. They will need the outside finances that the expatriate VDOs bring.

2. Expatriate Organizations:

The Niger government does not feel there is any great problem with defining NGOs, rather it is to get them to do longer term planning and program development. But, the government officials feel they have no criteria by which to judge the preferences of the VDOs, even as regards sectors of activity.

However, some of the international agency leaders asserted that problems do sometimes arise in categorizing the bi-lateral volunteer programs. The

German Volunteer program has faced this, for example, and resists being considered with the U.S. Peace Corps and wants to be treated as an NGO (or, in keeping with the subsequently adopted, new African terminology, VDO). The French "Association Française des voluntaires pour le Progrés" is a private organization, and also presents itself as an NGO, although the "Voluntaires pour la service nationale" is part of the official bi-lateral aid program.

Some of the prominent international agency leadership believes that there is no common body of thinking in Niger about what the PVOs should do, and that these organizations should diversify the levels and forms of their intervention, at the grass-roots, which is their traditional level, but also at the national and even the international levels. They should address the problems that attend the structural readjustment programs at the national level, for example. More generally, in their home countries and internationally, they should vigorously do what they can to sensitize the public and home governments, so as to address the debt problem, the problems of trade relations and the like, that so vitally affect the success of the local efforts of their own organizations and of the host governments alike.

3. Government Institutions:

The institutions of government that are to structure the "Société de Développement" are in place, although the officials we interviewed asserted that they still need to do a good deal of training of staff at all levels to make the system operate effectively.

At the national level, the second most important organ of the state is the "Conseil Nationale de Développement". This gives an overview of the plans. It engages in public education, giving seminars, symposiums, etc., on development at the base and helps to train and orient people in the technical ministries to work at the local levels. The particular ministries are responsible to make the necessary technical cadre available to work with local groups.

The representative and harmonizing structures at the intermediary and local levels are several. There are the "Conseil Régionale de Développement", the "Conseil Sous-Régionale de Développement", and the "Conseil villagoise de Développement".

At the very local level, that of the "micro-réalisation" efforts, there are only the VDOs and village cooperatives, GM etc. whether indigenous or external. If there is no VDO active in an area, the government will use the technical services of the state itself to carry out micro-realizations. Whether with VDOs or directly, there is an effort to achieve greater planning and harmonization. For example, for activities in the health field, the Ministry of Health has responsibility to provide assistance and to work at all levels from the Sous-Prefet up. They are responsible to inform all other ministries that might have an interest in the activity. All the different reports from the various administrative and representational bodies will be synthesized as low as the level of the Sous-prefet.

The Office of Micro-Realizations in the National Ministry of Planning would come into the picture at the end of the reporting line, and especially at the end of the project. That office is not responsible for project implementation or execution, which is for the "cadre de terrain", the local administrative staff, and the VDOs that have had a "protocol de mise en application" for a given project. The office will be deeply involved in the final evaluation of projects.

B. Government Perceptions about Spacial Location: This was not raised as a problem. The general system operates to spread activity around the country, and to respond to local pressures.

C. Government Perceptions about Procedures:

1. Registration/Authorization:

The Ministry of the Interior maintains a master-list of the authorized organizations. To get a general authorization, the requirements are that one bring a letter requesting permission, with details of the character of the organization and of the intended activities, in five copies, to the Ministry of Foreign Affairs and Cooperation. With this must also be five copies of the organizational statutes, minutes of the first meeting ever and of the last general assembly of the organization (the VDO leaders said it must be of the meeting where the decision was made to come to Niger). These are passed on to the Ministry of Plan, and the Ministry of Interior, for a response. Within fifteen days the organization is supposed to get an "arrêté" authorizing set up and the specific activities. This formality must be complied with. There is then issued a "Protocol typique" on the organization that authorizes it to carry on activity in the country and exempts it from customs and certain taxes. (Notice that no mention was made by these government officials of a requirement of the VDOs to walk the dossier around the technical ministries, implying that whatever approval from technical ministries is needed would be acquired by the Ministry of Interior itself. In practice, no doubt, the organizations find it useful to "chase" their own files.)

The Office of Micro-Realisation claims that the VDOs are completely free to have direct contact with local groups and to work up project proposals, but these must then fit into the local and higher planning frameworks. The Office maintains a "Project Bank" of project ideas and proposals that have come up the system from the local communities. The government is confident that the peasants can articulate their needs and desires, but points out that almost all the people at the local level are illiterate and are not able to elaborate the ideas into formal project proposals. They need the assistance of the VDO, or of the administrative cadre to do this. Thus, that projects may be presented to the VDOs by the government does not mean they are not expressions of the desires and felt needs of the people. The Government officials say they try to get the VDOs interested to take on these projects that local official bodies pass up the ladder to the national ministry, but typically only find such sponsors for a third of the project proposals they have in hand.

When the VDO has agreed on specific project commitments, this is embodied in a "protocol de mise en application" that is supposed to commit the organization and all the relevant services. These projects will have passed through the "comiteés de société de base" which must show that the project is its own, i.e., something it really wants, and that they possess the means necessary to implement it, especially in terms of the required manpower inputs. The project can then go to the "Conseil sous régionals" (sous-Préfet level) and then to" Conseil Régional" or "du Département" (at level of Préfet.)

The relationship between VDO and the Government is therefore described as a triangular one, with the VDO, local community bodies, and the state administrative apparatus all interacting.

2. Communications:

Especially during the period of most intense emergency, the Government conducted bi-weekly meetings, in which the VDOs, the various concerned ministries, and the bi-lateral and multi-lateral donors were represented. These gradually became less and less frequent until they have virtually ceased. The Ministry of Plan still sponsors various symposia and seminars, however, to assess the situation. At such a seminar held not long before our visit, we were told, stress was placed on the need for counter-season (dry season) agriculture. Such meetings produce minutes which then circulate throughout the government and GAP members.

Despite the close fit of planning and the bi-weekly meetings between GAP and the Government, or the periodic seminars and meetings with donors, the governmental ministries, especially the Ministry of Interior, complain that they are not able to trace the project activities of the VDOs. They seem constantly to want to know what the project objectives are and the general trends of their execution, including, how much money is involved in detail, so as to be able to report to the international agencies such as the IMF, in the financial projections they are called upon to make.

To the government officials with these responsibilities, it is especially important that the VDOs leaders and technicians touch base as they come in and out of the country or local area. They don't like things to wind up in newspaper photos of dying children.

3. Tax exemptions: None of the government officials raised this issue.

4. Freedom for the VDOs: The Government spokes-persons insisted that the VDOs are free to be in contact with local groups, and that they will make their own decisions about what projects to take on and what resources to commit to them.

5. Funding: The government officials that deal with VDOs say the problem is to find funding. They must look to the VDOs and the donors for support. They feel they offer lots more projects than are ever accepted, so they don't find funding for more than a third of them.

6. Plan Fit: All the machinery already described is designed to produce a good fit between the overall, long term Plan, and the activities and projects of the VDOs themselves. The government complains, however, that it is very difficult to get the VDOs to do longer term planning, and to make commitments over a sufficiently long period of time for their own planning operations to work well. They would like the VDOs to sign a funding commitment for a three-year period, to commit themselves to a specified amount of financial and other support. The members of GAP argue that this is not possible for them.

There is also the problem of having the VDOs have flexibility of activity, so that they can adapt to the different regions of the country, which have different needs and mentalities. The government periodically holds seminars and meetings to deal with issues such as project design, or how to calculate the production of a project. However, government officials also say they would like to have greater uniformity of the process of planning, despite their stated desire to see the organizations better adapted to particular areas.

D. Government Officials' Perceptions of Problems with VDOs:

1. Tax: this issue was not raised.

2. Attention/Tolerance of VDOs by Government: The Government has included VDOs in its various meetings with donors, and in the planning process. They regard this as an important sector.

3. Other -- Early Warning System:

Some of the prominent international agency officials felt that the Government resents the early warning system because it may involve sensitive issues of their relations with neighboring states. Refugees in Niger from Algeria or Libya were discussed as a problem, as are, even, Niger refugees in Nigeria, etc. Often the recipient country wants these people to leave, but does not want to bear the onus of kicking them out, and so it attempts to have the United Nations handle the problem. The source country may not want an early return of such refugee populations, because of the lack of resources to apply to the problem of adapting and relocating them. One may wonder how the early warning systems are going to work in practice over the long run.

4. Other -- United Support of Artists for Africa (USAFA) and Live Aid/ Band Aid:

International agency officials said they thought the USAFA (the sponsors of the "We Are the World" record) funding selection process worked smoothly enough. The initial meeting to inform groups of the opportunity and the guidelines was held under the auspices of the Ministry of Plan itself, and then much of the communication was handled by UNDP. But there did develop a sense of competition and of "turf" that did upset some of the international agency circles and possibly the government. Government officials claimed they had sometimes faced similar problems, of VDOs from the source country of the funding thinking they should be THE only channel of its application.

International agency officials reported that there had been considerable dissatisfaction with the Live Aid/Band Aid operation. They had no guidelines, and there was no move here to use the guidelines from the USAFA. Feeling that the LA/BA operation had been deceptive was so intense that the UNDP attempted to draw away from any involvement with it. A committee was established for considering applications to LA/BA, that included government officials, and that set up quite a lot of meetings for Mr. Geldof and others of the organization, but in the end the organization did not fund any program in Niger.

5. Other -- Transfer of Unemployment:

Niger Government officials expressed the view that, with so many indigenous university graduates unable to find employment, even with the
VDO/NGO sector, that the external NGOs were essentially merely "importing their unemployment into Niger". They felt that many, if not most, of the
expatriate staff of the local operations of international NGOs, and government sponsored volunteer programs, lack genuine professional training, and
thus were really no better qualified, technically, than the local graduates.
They want this to stop. They argued that the NGOs should hire the local
youth, and that there is real potential for the youth to organize themselves
into VDO groups, although this has not yet advanced very far.

E. Government Perceptions of Prospects

1. General Funding: Only the UNDP spoke of possibilities of expanded
funding for the VDO sector. They like VDOs because of their efficiency, but
want to see them work better with governments, and look at larger scale
efforts. The UNDP was trying to round up project proposals for the second
funding cycle of the USAFA. There is a prospect of a Round Table Conference of Donors that could include, and certainly profit, VDOs. The main
meetings of this sort are in Geneva. They expect a follow-up meeting in
Niger.

2. Umbrella and on-granting facilities: The UNDP foresees prospects
of umbrella regional projects in the Sahel, that might include Niger, but did
not mention this prospect as based in Niger. Rather, the lead seems to be
coming from Dakar, Senegal.

CASE STUDY TWO -- BURKINA FASO

I. Introduction

Under the leadership of Captain Thomas Sankara, Burkina Faso (B.F.) was distinctive in its approach to and experience with VDO activity. We judge the pattern of policy and approach that was presented to us during visits in February and May of 1987, to be the likely model on which other Sahelian states will eventually converge. No doubt, even before the tragic assassination of Sankara, there were processes of evolution underway that might have changed the patterns we assess here. With the October 1987 coup and demise of Sankara and a number of other high officials, the policies and practices of the country may change very significantly, although the new top leadership was long associated with the former regime, and may attempt to continue the previous policies, or even to purify them. All of our comments are based on the pattern that obtained prior to Sankara's death.

The interesting elements of the situation in B.F. are:
1) it and the region around it are poor, Sahelian, and hard hit by the effects of drought; 2) it has attracted a number of the more important external VDOs in recent years, some of which may now have left for other nearby countries; 3) there are a number of experienced and productive indigenous VDOs; 4) the VDO community is well organized within itself; 5) the state also has well organized structures to monitor, guide, represent and respond to VDO activities and interests; and 6) the state bureau dealing with VDOs has good access to the highest levels of authority; 7) the personal qualities of leadership of both the state and the VDO agencies that represented the two sides of the government-VDO nexus, in Sankara's period, were exceptionally high, and 8) the state leadership in general, and its policies, seem genuinely devoted to empowering the masses and advancing them. However, much of this configuration of elements depends on the particular people in the principal leadership positions, especially on the state side, and could change drastically with their replacement.

Despite these elements, which we see as unusual strengths, there are somewhat serious problems arising from disparities of perspective and perception between the two communities: state and VDO, and possibly also within the VDO community. The weakness of governmental structures, due to lack of financing, and perhaps to the inevitable problems of consolidating "revolutionary" redirection in an African society, causes difficulties for the VDOs that attempt to carry out programs at local levels in relation to state structures that are malfunctioning or in flux.

Burkina Faso itself is a country with very limited financial resources and rather rudimentary development of its economic infrastructure. The country was very hard hit by both the droughts of the 70s and the 80s. It has needed substantial relief assistance, and is in constant need of external financing for its development program. Serious efforts are being made, however, to maximize the use of both natural and human local resources.

Also, Burkina Faso depends on the remittances of a large number of its citizens who have migrated elsewhere, especially to Cote d'Ivoire, for employment. Much of the abler and more energetic leadership for grass roots activity is among the emigrants.

II. VDO Leadership Perceptions

A. VDO Leadership Perceptions About the Actors -- People/Products:

1. Indigenous Organizations:

The VDO community is well organized into the "Secrétariat des Organisations non-gouvernementales" (SPONG) which was established in 1976. It has fifty-two (52) members, about half of which are indigenous, out of a possible total of about 150 in the country. The organization has come to be accepted as the representative of the VDOs, and initially was a central source of information for all the VDOs. There have been other consortiums than SPONG, and there are non members, (e.g., the "Association Française des voluntaires pour le Progrès", "Croix rouge", ADAUA are all not members of SPONG). Obviously some of these non-members are organizations with rather large programs. The government's listing of VDOs with the larger programs that have been incorporated in the Development Plan numbers 72. Dues requirements are not the likely cause for the resistance of these organizations, as annual dues are only 50,000CFA (about $150 in mid 1987). SPONG believes that any of the organizations could afford this level, and if an indigenous organization made a case of hardship, even that could be reduced. The development and expansion of SPONG may have been hurt by the establishment of an effective Government bureau, the "Bureau de suivi des Organisation non-gouvernementales" (BSONG), in the Presidency (discussed further on).

SPONG leadership points out that there are 7500 village groups that are not expected to be members of the organization. The SPONG leadership tries various methods of contact and concertation with the member organizations, and tries to promote the regrouping of villages. The federation cannot include every one of these little village organizations. A prerequisite for membership in SPONG is that the organization's objectives not be limited to working in one single corner of the country; they have to be ready to go everywhere.

The SPONG has a permanent staff of six people. The staff is headed by a full-time Executive Director, who is a dedicated, articulate, reasonably well-educated young man of substantial experience in grass-roots development work in the field. There is also a Secretary General who receives an honorarium for his part-time service to the organization, and whom others among the VDO leadership think takes very seriously this leadership role. Additionally he has his own professional work as a religious minister, and heads an active and successful VDO associated with his church organization, the Federation of Evangelical Churches (FEME). (This person was elected Treasurer of the new continent-wide FAVDO). The FEME has built a number of dams and water resource installations around the country, partially with USA for Africa funding.

It is generally believed that, other than the church organizations, perhaps, all the indigenous VDOs depend on external allies and sponsors for their finances. Initially, they admit, they tended to report only to these external affiliates. Also, the BSONG acknowledges the problem of uneven distribution of activity around the country and claims to be concerned to achieve a more even balance in this regard. Their sense of priority activity needs are: reforestation, resettlement of displaced persons through the creation of new villages, or their reintegration into their old locations, with new employment generating and production activities.

2. Expatriate Organizations: People/ Products

We have noted that some of the non-members of SPONG are substantial organizations. Some of these are expatriate (French volunteers program, for example.) The Red Cross Committee and the ADAUA are both local organizations, although the former is affiliated with the International Red Cross.

Almost all the major American and European VDOs that have programs in the Sahel are represented in Burkina Faso. Despite the perception in other countries that there was an exodus of such organizations from B.F. following the Sankara revolution in 1983, recent accounting of organizational activity seem to indicate their continued presence. None of our discussions with VDO leadership raised any evidence of an intention on the part of an external VDO to leave the country. The Peace Corps, on the other hand, is now winding down its activity in the country, having been encouraged to leave due to reaction to U.S. policy and actions elsewhere in Africa; and, in any case, the program was suffering from budgetary cut backs.

The experience of the USA for AFRICA (USAFA) funding process was one of the first experiences with all the groups coming together, say the leaders of some of those who participated. This committee process involved, first, a general meeting open to any interested party, to convey the guidelines and procedures of the funding, convened by someone the USAFA had asked to be their local liaison person/organization. In Burkina Faso that organization was the Save the Children Foundation (SCF). The same committee and the USAFA guidelines were used to recommend projects for funding by the Live Aid/ Band Aid organization, which had provided no specific guidelines. See more on the process under Special Issues further on.

3. Governmental Agencies:

The SPONG had asked that there be a ministry of contact or "tutelle" in order to organize and "rationalize" the VDO contacts with the government. Of course they also wanted to guard the autonomy of the VDOs. At the beginning of 1976, The Ministry of Rural Development had a person designated to be the contact. Problems with contacts with the other ministries were supposed to be taken to this person. This procedure was changed in 1983, when Sankara brought this function into the Prime Minister's office. In '84, he brought it into the Presidency, as the "Bureau de Suivi des Organisations non-gouvernementales" (BSONG).

During our visits there was also in existence under the Minister of "Essor Familial" (Family Assistance) an Interministerial Committee for Drought relief, that coordinates relief assistance. The government is becoming more clear about what they want specifically from the VDOs and what its goals and rules are for them, as revealed in their presentations to the "Seance de Reflexion" of SPONG.

B. VDO Leadership Perceptions About Place:

In our discussions, the VDO leaders were not very concerned about the spacial allocation of their activities because the VDOs think there are few if any official guide lines for their activity, other than the general priorities emphasized in the national Plan. They view themselves as rather dispersed around the country, and assume that the government thinks that is a bad thing. We should note that in most other countries, the complaint is the opposite, that the VDOs are concentrated in a few places, leaving many others under-serviced. One of the leaders of a large organization said that formerly the VDOs each seemed to have their own favorite local development organization to which they related. That resulted in some regions being left uncovered. There has also been some multiplication of efforts without sufficient harmonization. SPONG leadership feels strongly that there must be some VDO activity everywhere throughout the country.

C. VDO Leadership Perceptions About Procedures:

1. Registration / Authorization:

The VDO leadership believes that each organization now has to get a general protocol of authorization, so there is more structure being put into place for the VDOs than in the 1970s. There is also the Bureau de Suivi des ONG (BSONG) and new regulations regarding quarterly and annual reporting, including forms to be completed indicating budgets, program plans, relevance of their operations to the government's objectives.

2. Communication:

Some of the VDO leadership believes that there is more interaction now among the VDOs, and with the international donor agencies. They say that the SPONG, back in the 1970s, was *the* central source of information of the sort that is now provided by BSONG and they question, therefore, its role now. It is felt by groups like the Save the Children Foundation (SCF) that the UNDP, UNICEF, and even the FAO are getting out more and connecting with other organizations. In the USAFA funding process they did get some conflict between the UNDP and the designated USAFA liaison person (SCF rep) which could have been divisive, but they worked it out.

Some of the leaders of individual VDOs seem to be well informed about the other VDOs and Burkina Faso institutions that exist to deal with the VDOs. There are now some general meetings of the VDOs (once a year?) that serve the same function that the USAFA selection committee served in pulling the groups together and providing for a communications link between them.

3. Taxes and Duties: None of the VDO leadership mentioned this as a problem.

4. Freedom for VDOs: At least one prominent VDO leader questioned whether the VDOs really have to do only what the government may want. Even with the BSONG, and the requirement to report each three months,

and the possibility they could be kicked out if they are not following their stated program, that program itself is not imposed.

5. Funding:

One of the external VDOs, the Oxfam-U.K., believes that in 1986 about $65m came to Burkina Faso through the VDOs. It is thought that then there were up to 150 such organizations. Some of the regions did not have much in the way of program because they had not attracted VDOs, due most probably to the lack of effective "Organisations régionales de développement" (ORDs) in those regions.

6. Fit with the Plan:

The VDOs had an input into the Five-Year Plan, especially at the local level in selecting projects and targets. There was a general meeting between them and the Ministry of the Plan.

At a local level they related to the relevant "organisation rurale de développement" (ORD). The VDOs have had a lot of problems developing and carrying out programs at the local level because of the requirement they work within the framework provided by the ORD, which themselves have had many problems. The Burkina Faso government has now decided to dismantle the whole system, in order to decentralize to an even more local level; but this decision had not yet been implemented.

The Burkina Faso Government asked some of the VDOs to set up settlement camps for the many persons displaced because of the drought. External assistance did come for this activity, and groups like the Oxfam-UK had substantial programs. This has become a controversial question, however, discussed at greater length below under "Special Issues."

Another issue that has become somewhat controversial in other countries, but not yet so in Burkina Faso, concerns an early warning system established among the VDOs to warn of impending drought and/or famine. The SCF and the Oxfam-UK have co-funded such a system, that is not yet in place (it will take five years to complete) that involves government- conducted studies at the village level, in key sample villages, and individuals in *each* village who would report some basic data to monitors on a variety of socio-economic indicators and movement of population in general and pastoralists in particular, agricultural prices, etc. rather than just nutritional status. All the Oxfam field offices will also do research for this early warning system.

D. VDO Perceptions About Problems:

1. Tax Exemption: This was not raised as an issue.

2. Government Attention and Tolerance:

This also was not raised as an issue. Generally the VDOs seem to accept the idea that the Burkina Faso revolution is real and reflects an effort to do something effective at the local levels. They also noted the government's intimate involvement in the early warning system.

3. Special Funding: This was not raised as an issue.

4. Special Issues -- Refugees and Displaced Persons:

With severe drought in many areas of the North of the country, and in other neighboring Sahelian countries, there are many refugees and displaced persons coming into the cities, and into village areas of lesser hardship.

The government and the SPONG had meetings of the VDOs on the issue. The SPONG leadership claimed that it was the administrative authorities who were first to want to create the camps.   They had received relief support from external donors for that. An investigatory team was sent through the North to determine the needs and the capacities of the people, which led to an agreed on "grande lignes d'orientation", a basic approach that rejected concentrating people in camps, which was what the VDOs preferred. That approach was thought to lead to the problem of leaving some people out. Rather, SPONG thought it better to organize the people in order to reintegrate them into their own villages or integrate them into other villages.

By and large, the people concerned wanted to stay together, and or-ganize. There was the matter of preserving their traditions. Also there was danger within the camps. However, those who were left in the old villages were subjected to famine, which led also to dependence. Therefore, the SPONG wanted to find out what one could do at the place of origin. They felt the need to orient the VDOs to do something there. Some regrouping of displaced people in new locations has occurred, while some remained in the village without any means of livelihood. For the short run the SPONG got the VDOs to organize the distribution and resale of the food relief supplies to people wherever they were scattered, and assist them to overcome the difficulties of transporting these supplies.

In the discussion among the VDOs, some thought that one should not invest more in the Northern drought zones. Rather, one should go to the

South, in order to avoid having the South become just like the North, i.e., to start to do something in the zones still good for agriculture so   that desertification would not spread into the areas of the South. Others said one should replant in the North; or, instead of working in the South, go to the West. A consensus was found -- it would be good to do both, replant in North, do new development in South, but there must be some activity everywhere. For example, there is not a lot of activity in the Central districts, and one can still stop the advance of the desert there. It is not yet at a crucial phase, but has already started to degrade, due to deforestation, cultivation, and cutting for construction.

The SPONG leadership feels it still has to struggle to convince some displaced groups to accept integration into existing villages or new settlements outside of camps. This would require that many of them learn new fashions of living, and of cultivation. They are also trying to convince the VDOS to work everywhere. They just don't know enough about what the future might bring; perhaps one should not condemn them, argued one SPONG leader, "la vrais condemnation n'est pas à leur," -- they are not the real ones to blame.   They need help and advice.

E. VDO Perceptions of Prospects

1. Funding -- Special Issues:

a. USAFA and LA/BA:

The prospect for new USAFA funding caused a general review of the experience. As was noted above, there was some duplication of and a good many problems with communications from the USAFA headquarters and field representatives. The official Liaison Person for linking the USAFA operation with the field-based groups, the local Director for SCF, was not getting all the information coming to the UNDP Res. Rep., and vice versa. It could have caused great divisiveness.

The liaison person from SCF, felt the process worked well on balance. About $10m of projects were identified. A problem with the preparation of proposals developed because the groups were initially told they had only ten days in which to submit them. Even so, many were well done. There were only a few persistent turf battles. They were finally able to agree on priorities, although there was some duplication of effort among the VDOs. There could have been serious conflict, but the UNDP representative played a mediating role, and several times pulled back proposals they had put forward, in order to let other groups into the picture, and then took up any slack left at the end. There was what the SCF thought was a good balance between local and external VDOs and between European and American ones.

Local leaders felt the USAFA procedures were more helpful than those of the Live Aid/Band Aid group. Indeed, the USAFA was the only one to give specific (and they thought reasonable) guidelines, so these were applied to the LA/BA as well. Bob Geldof's visit had gone rather badly, however, as his bruskness and arrogance sparked a lot of resentment locally, although it did stimulate more energetic coordination. Mr. Geldof's visit to B.F. engendered considerable tension, and ultimately resulted in a special mission to London to work out funding decisions. Initially, LA/BA rejected almost every proposal submitted, 25 out of the 27. The Mission (which included the Secretary-General of SPONG and the Director of the BSONG) were told that projects involved in building dams had been rejected because this would only produce more mosquitos. Finally about 17 proposals were accepted. There were also complaints that LA/BA made the promised recipients wait for their money, whereas USAFA support came through almost immediately, for those who received it at all.

The special selection committee from the first USAFA and LA/BA funding cycle was continued, and, based in the SPONG, it has become a sort of management committee, to oversee the disbursement of LA/BA funds as the projects show they have used previous receipts well.

For the second cycle of USAFA funding of recovery and development projects, the Request for Proposals of which were received around April, with a June deadline, emphasis was given to communicating with the indigenous VDOs. USAFA later indicated that these proposals could be submitted in French. The committee for the second cycle of USAFA funding is composed of the SPONG Executive Director, plus the BSONG, the SCF (who sits as current Chair of the SPONG) the UNICEF, and a local VDO that does training, the CESAO. The VDOs were called together in a meeting and the new brochures circulated. This committee did not attempt to select among the proposals however. Those that seemed in order were sent on to USAFA.

b. Special Issue - External Funding Abuse of Local VDOs:

The experience of the local Partnership for Productivity (P.f.P.) affiliate was especially grievous. They had built up quite an impressive program for small-scale enterprise, with a credit facility (average loans were about $270) for entrepreneurs in five sectors including: agriculture, transport, commercial transport, artisanry and herding. They also operated a substantial vehicle repair garage, the only one in the vicinity and successful enough to meet some of the recurrent costs of the rest of the program. The organization submitted a proposal to USAFA for a reinforcement activity which had begun in 1984 and involved assistance for access to markets, additional loans, equipment, and counsel. A second phase of this operation was to provide some vehicles and tractors and assistance to three seed enterprises.

The proposal was funded but the money, somehow, was sent to the headquarters organization in Washington D.C. which, itself, was already in financial trouble and, allegedly, had misused funds from other sources. The USAFA funds were used mostly by the Headquarters to pay their bills there, and still they were in such deep financial trouble that the U.S. government shut it down. The field operation received only a very small portion of the USAFA funds that had been awarded to it and thus the whole P.f.P. program in Burkina Faso was put into severe jeopardy. The USAID felt a particular responsibility for the P.f.P. program and arranged for CARE to take the operation over for two 90 day periods, beginning December 1986, to give them time to find a new parent organization.

At the time of our visit it was not clear how the P.f.P. program would recover. Subsequently, support was made available from several American organizations. One external supporter, the William Penn Foundation, whose support helped tide them over, required that they be linked to an international PVO. However, the Council for International Development (U.S. based) and the USAFA continued to express an interest in their operations only if they could develop a credible program for full registration as a local organization, with indigenization of their governing board, and ultimately of their leadership. The BSONG was helping them to accomplish that. Given the P.f.P. plans for such changes, their proposal to USAFA for second-round funding was successful.

This is an especially important case because the field program was not at fault, was working in a region where no other VDO was operating, had brought its credit program to maturity where the borrowers were paying back their loans. All that was put in jeopardy not because of the poor performance of locals in the field, but for poor performance by the Headquarters leadership of one of the more experienced, well-known and established international VDOs. Clearly, not all the problems of good management and performance fall on the side of the indigenous VDOs.

III.Perceptions by Burkina Faso Government and International Agency Officials

A. Government Perceptions Regarding the Actors -- People / Products:

   1. Indigenous Organizations:

Government, as represented by its chief official charged with relations with the VDOs, was strikingly forthright in both its criticism of the level of VDO development reached in B.F., and in praise of the advantages VDOs offer. The SPONG was called a "point of weakness", for example. It is considered to have a structure to regroup the VDOs but the members of it act too much like a club. Also, even though it has a program of its own, and a secretariat, it doesn't really have financing and so is dependent. The SPONG cannot really discipline its members, who as a group, were thought to be especially undisciplined. Agencies like the SPONG, and even the BSONG itself, can only represent these organizations, and find it hard really to coordinate them.

The issue of dependency was emphasized in several ways in the assessment of the VDO sector, especially the indigenous ones. They all depend on external financing, in the view of the BSONG. The potential for a truly local financial base for these organizations is low, given that the "solvent" class in the rural areas constitutes only about one percent of the population. Few if any of these groups are thought to be able to make their assistance programs self-sufficient. So each organization and group winds up with its own alliances. These organizations are likely to find the current program of promoting the use of indigenous resources hard going, as they have to search for supplies in B.F.

At the level of the individual organization, some indigenous and external VDOs have come in for rather stringent criticism by Government. Some of the organizations, especially indigenous ones, were accused of having been bogus (and indeed, one, but only one, such was ever "déjugée" and ordered disbanded) and others of carrying out fraudulent activity, especially with the resale of grains and food relief and supplies. They have also had to be warned from time to time not to get involved in local political debates.

On the other hand, the BSONG emphasized the advantages offered by VDOs, including their non-bureaucratic nature and a capacity for quick, flexible and dedicated action. There are still problems in agreeing on appropriate definitions for these organizations however. Not only was this mentioned in our interviews, but on several occasions during official meetings between the VDOs and Government (such as during the First Working Meeting Between the BSONG and the NGOs of 14/15 May, 1984). [36] This takes on a special character in Burkina Faso because not only is there the

---

[36] Cf. "Compte Rendu, Premiere Rencontre de Travail entre BSONG et ONG, 14 et 15 Mai, 1984." p. 2.

problem of how to treat the many village level self-help activities and group-ings, but there is also the question of what status to give to the Regional Development Associations and Committees that were spawned as part of the present and previous governmental programs. BSONG has been especially critical of the "freezing of their activity" by the regional associations following the Sankara-led coup of 1983 and the inauguration of the present revolution-ary programs.

The BSONG also expressed concern that the VDOs may become over-loaded with demands and expectations, especially from the local people, that they simply could not be expected to handle.

2. Expatriate VDOs:

In the estimation of the BSONG, the VDOs are too often jealous of their autonomy. It makes it really hard to coordinate their activities at the national level. Following the 1983 period of ecological crisis, and the change of government, there was an influx of organizations which operated in a free-for-all atmosphere. The assistance they brought was appreciated so there was great tolerance, but one saw quite a lot of organizations stumbling over each other, with disputes over "rights of first occupancy" as if a new "Scramble for Africa" were going on. There was also "des piètinements" -- marching in place. Local politicians started chasing after this or that organization and resource, and cultivated favors of the VDOs. This inevitably produced uneven coverage and results.

The BSONG believes that some of the external VDOs also shared in the corruptions of the old pre-revolutionary order, with cheating, and marketing of relief supplies etc. At the start, the BSONG felt it had to threaten these organizations, to get them straightened out and working in harmony with others and with the government. The organizations did not want to make the proper contacts with government and administrative officials, saying that this just wasted their time. But, in Africa, the BSONG leadership argued, the formalities of stopping in on the Prefet etc. is important. "The external organizations were sometimes acting as if they were in conquered territory."

The VDOs have to develop a more coordinated and harmonized, concer-tized approach, thinks the BSONG. This was not expressed as a criticism of external connections. The many partners from abroad are judged to be necessary, as few of the local activities can be self financing, in terms of the central operations. But they do think that at the project level more of it could be "pasteurse" (profitable) at least for the peasants involved, in order to lift them to a higher standard of living. But the organizations themselves will need subsidies. The bureau wondered if the organizations couldn't build in income-generating activities for themselves. The VDOs seem to want to be initiators but not workers. Sometimes also, these organizations get framed-in by their own activity and can't seem to see the larger picture.

3. Governmental Agencies:

The self perception of the BSONG and other governmental institutions in terms of their role and prerogatives has changed somewhat during the course of recent years. In the first meeting between the Government and the VDOs, held in June 1984, the BSONG representative described the functions of his office as including "Coordonner les activite's des ONG sur toute l'étendue du territoire. -- Intégrer ces activités dans une politique globale cohérente en rapport avec les activités des services de l'État." (Coordinate the activities of the NGOs throughout the country; Integrate these activities in a coherent general policy in relation to the activities and services of the state." [37] This was meant to imply a decisive role in controlling the NGOs. Yet, it was quickly discovered that the VDO organizations would resist such coordination and control. The BSONG backed off of that line and in subsequent meetings, and in our interviews, it was stressed that the Bureau's role would be to "represent" and facilitate the work of the VDOs.

In the minutes of a subsequent, 1986 meeting between the Government and the VDOs, the coordination function was dropped from the list of its responsibilities. The responsibilities of the office are given as:

"--Integrate and orient the NGO activities in a coherent global policy in
    keeping with national priorities.
--Facilitate exchange of experience among the NGOs them selves, and
    between them and the state services of all sorts, and develop and
    dynamic of functional collaboration.
--Gather statistics from the NGOs to permit planning and an accounting
    of these organization's investments within the overall national planning
    process.
--Participate in the development of NGO programs.
--See that each NGO project is monitored by the relevant ministry.
--Monitor and evaluate the NGO programs in the field, either by the
    Bureau itself, or by the competent ministry.

---

[37] "Compte Rendu de la Réunion du 6 Juin 1984, Portant Sur les Questions Relatives Aux O.N.G.," Conseil National de La Révolution, Présidence de la République, BSONG.

--Determine the places of intervention for NGOs, taking into account the activities of other organizations and of the felt needs at the regional level.
--Disqualify NGOs if their activity is against the interest of the people." [38]

In our interview, the BSONG director stressed that "my own office is not a bureau of direction. I do not have the right to give them (NGOs) directives, but I can monitor them and advise them to organize better, and as Burkinabé NGOs, and to add an Administrative Council and have personnel in the field. I do have to intervene often, but if there are good intentions to uplift the economy, and a dynamism in the grass roots activities, then we are satisfied."

The BSONG felt a responsibility to help the state use its limited resources wisely, to invest in such a way as not to be crushed. The state has no money for equipment, for example. Yet the state input is substantial, taking into account the tax exemptions etc., such that about a third of the value of these operations is provided by the state. This all means that they should work to orient the VDOs such that their activities would profit the peasants themselves, and to invest the resources they have so that the donations they had received would continue. But they would have to make hard choices. They should concentrate their investments where it can be most effective, where the peasants have already developed a high level of consciousness. Most of the effort to identify the goals and means of development occurs at the level of the Comité de Base. One must assess the resources available at the level of the provinces.

B. Government Perceptions about Spacial Location of VDO Activity:

The BSONG expressed concern that areas of the country not be neglected, as a result of each VDO having its own favorite local ally among the ORD, or politicians. The official view of what would define a VDO (NGO) and set it apart from the village organizations or regional associations was that its orientation and program would be national in scope.

Yet, spacial location of activity was not stressed as an issue. There was more criticism of the indigenous ORD and ARD (Associations régionales de développement) than the VDOs. It seems generally to be assumed that if

---

[38] "Création et L'Fonctionnement du Bureau de Suivi des O.N.G. à La Présidence du Faso," Conseil National de la Révolution, Présidence du Faso. 23 Juillet, 1986.

there is proper "concertation" among the VDOs and between them and the state, the spacial spread of their activity would accord with Plan priorities and felt needs. A report of a meeting of BSONG with the VDOs (the most recent such meeting held prior to our visit in May 1987) does not make much of the issue of even spread around the country, but does note that there had been progressive movement from "interventions isolées" to ones that were within "un cadre de cohèrence." [39]

C. Government Perceptions about Procedures:

1. Registration/Authorization:

Neither our interviews nor the documentation available on the history of the work of BSONG reveal any particular problem with regard to the registration or authorization of the VDOs. It was evident that the BSONG has the authority to recommend disqualification of a VDO (domestic or external) but it has actually done so only in one case, where an indigenous organization was judged to be bogus, with no real field operation.

2. Communication:

Two meetings are held each year between the government ministries and the VDOs, arranged by the BSONG. These "séances de réflexion" can treat particular sectors or topics, such as the health programs, treated in the January 1987 meeting, or can be more general in orientation. These meetings give the government a chance to present its policy orientations, as well as hear of the commitments and concerns of the VDOs.

There have been such seances where ministries concerned with a given aspect of VDO activity that was discussed were not present at the meeting. The VDOs have been vocal in their criticism about such absences, and have pushed the BSONG to correct the deficiency. The VDOs have also not hesitated to call for the ministries to present well worked out proposals when calling for the commitment of the VDOs for their implementation.

The BSONG generally ignored the issue raised with us by some VDO leaders that the BSONG had, without intention, made it more difficult for the SPONG to grow and serve its functions, because now individual VDOs could go directly to the Bureau for the information and services previously the domain of the SPONG.

------

[39] "Rencontre de Travail entre BSONG et ONG le 6 Avril 1987." p.1.

At the time of our visit, the government was emphatic about needing to receive regular (three month and annual) reports from the VDOs and threatened to disqualify or expel those which fail to provide them.

3. Tax and Import Duty Exemptions:

This issue has occasioned considerable discussion among the VDOs and between them and the government. In the June 1984 meeting it was pointed out that there was considerable confusion about existing regulations and that the various texts and laws needed to be consolidated. The customs regime was called chaotic, even by the government officials. It was also felt that the issue of how to define the VDOs (NGOs) was relevant because the various regulations providing for import duty exemptions etc. refer to specific types of organizations. Nonetheless, the two questions were kept separate, and an Interministerial Commission that was already working on the issue of the tax and duty regulations was charged with the problem of consolidating and clarifying the existing rules, and the BSONG asked to propose needed modifications. [40] It has been noted in various BSONG presentations that the combined effect of tax and import duty exonerations and direct inputs of equipment and infrastructure (which seem generally to be very limited) constitute a third of the value of the development program of the VDO sector.

The "Convention Cadre d'Établissement" (Framework Convention for Establishing an NGO) provides that the state will "facilitate the entry and stay of any foreign citizens engaged by the organization to carry out its programs", and for the exoneration of all taxes and duties except operational taxes on vehicles, and taxes on arms, cattle imports and certain use fees. Equipment and vehicles used in their development work can be imported duty free. Personal and professional effects can be brought in under franchise, if within six months of the owner's arrival in the country.

4. Freedom for VDOs:

During the Sankara period, at least, the Burkina Faso Government presented itself as a genuine and exemplary champion of VDO-type development; the BSONG asserts that the state really appreciates the role of the VDOs. This fits in the grass-roots revolutionary program of assisting the peasants to have a better life, and the emphasis on mobilization of local resources to accomplish this.

---

[40] Compte Rendu...6 Juin 1984, *op. cit.*, p. 2.

Although the BSONG has sometimes pressured and "menaced" the VDO community to promote more coordination of effort and greater contact with the administration, it has also played an active role in representing the interests of the VDO community to the various organs of government. Indeed, perhaps ironically, the status of the bureau and of its Director rises with the growth and good performance of the VDOs and it is therefore in its interests to promote just that. The Bureau also has attempted to publicize and make more visible the amount of development investment and assistance handled by the VDO sector. It therefore collected the statistics on program action from the various VDOs and published them in a "Programme Previsionnel des O.N.G." in order to have the government understand the substantial size of the VDO resource pool. It was also an effort to get the VDOs to carry out longer term planning and to commit them to substantial levels of future contributions.

5. Funding: The BSONG had little to say about funding opportunities for the VDO sector. There is little expectation of local financing for this activity, other than the Government's contribution through waived fees, duties and taxes.

6. Plan Fit:

A lot of effort has gone into bringing the VDO sector into the Plan, and to achieving a common coherent framework of planning and action between the VDO and the governmental efforts. The "Programme Previsionnel des O.N.G." for the years 1986-1990 foresees a total contribution from these organizations of about 35 billion CFA (over $100m) for the five-year period, based on projections that, no doubt, are *not* reliable commitments from the organizations. Even so, that many of the organizations have predicted such substantial future programs does exert a bit of pressure on them, and becomes at least a goal to be striven for. The harder figure of the value of VDO contributions in 1986 of about 9.5 billion CFA (over $30 m) is also impressive in the context of one of the world's poorer economies.

The sectoral distribution of the present and projected inputs seems to accord well with the policy orientation of the BFG. BSONG noted, in its presentation to the 6 April, 1987 Working Meeting between the Government ministries and the VDOs, that the sectoral distribution would be as follows:

-- Food Assistance   28%
-- Agriculture   26%
-- Water Resource Development   23%
-- Health   10%
-- Artisanal (crafts)   4%
-- National Education   2%

-- Miscellaneous   5%

The BSONG representative claimed that these allocations accorded well with the state priorities in both letter and spirit, especially with respect to the emphasis on agriculture and water resource development. He called on the VDOs to hold to their pledges and to this orientation.

The government has attempted to guide the VDOs in specific sectoral and programmatic directions at a number of the meetings that have been held to bring the ministries and agencies together with the VDOs. For example, in September of 1984 a meeting was held to present the government's program to achieve 250 new water reservoirs around the country, and its desire that the VDOs carry out the program within a fifteen-month period. The VDO were concerned to have the government know that they could not commit themselves to finish such dam and reservoir projects within a fifteen-month period (saying that in reality it would probably take two years). The VDOs also pointed out that projects of this sort would really require the enthusiastic support of the population who would have to do most of the work. It was in this meeting, also, that the VDOs pointed to the need for the government to present individual project plans that were clear, complete and feasible, if they were to succeed in raising the money for them abroad. The BSONG did carry that message to Government, concluding its report on the session by saying "the ball is therefore in the court of the new Minister of Water Resources." [41]

Generally the government and the BSONG have pushed for "concertation" which they interpret as "joint, close planning and harmonization of actions with those of the official structures." Other more particular points that have been put forward recently as governmental expectations from the VDO sector include:

--help with "grande chantiers" larger (state? or communal?) farms, with "food for work" or other such contributions to canteens for the workers on these farms;
--local purchase (within Burkina Faso or, where necessary, elsewhere in Africa) of food stuffs for such programs;
--local purchase of utensils and other project inputs;
--five-year projects of plans and funding commitments.

---

[41] Compte Rendue de la rencontre du BSONG avec les ONG, les 25 et 26 Sept., 1984. p. 4.

D. Government Perceptions of Problems:

1. Tax and Duties: There were no persistent special concerns in this regard.

2. Attention/ tolerance: We have already pointed to the government's conviction that it is a champion of an approach to development that would emphasize VDO type organizations and activity.

3. Other: USAFA funding and follow-up. They would like to see the USAFA use a management committee like the one used to supervise the disbursements for the Live Aid/ Band Aid funding. The BSONG seems to have preferred the disbursement arrangements that were finally worked out with Live Aid/ Band Aid whereby the money passed through the Selection Committee (now become the Management Committee) that was based in the SPONG and included BSONG. The initial disbursement was 40% of the award, with a subsequent evaluation and monitoring by the Committee before the remaining disbursements were made. This not only enhanced the role of the Committee, but made the recipients more careful about their accounting practices. The USAFA, on the other hand, sent the disbursements directly to the recipients.

E. Government Perceptions about Prospects:

1. General Funding: There were no thoughts about how VDOs could develop new sources of funding.

2. On-Granting Arrangements: This was an interesting and attractive idea which they would like to explore further. They thought that, perhaps, some sort of local foundation could be established to support the kind of work VDOs are carrying out.

3. New Areas/ Activities: The FAVDO:

Our interviews occurred before the FAVDO conference in Dakar, at which the Director of the BSONG would be a principal speaker. At the time of our visit to Burkina Faso he did not have high expectations from the meeting. There was criticism that with money so limited perhaps it should not be spent on grand meetings. Rather, he argued, the resources available should be put directly to work in the field.

It was also pointed out that prior efforts to organize such international federations and servicing agencies had failed. With the political problems of some of the organizers of the Dakar Conference, one wondered if this would not turn out to be just another meeting.

There was the feeling that one cannot really coordinate the VDOs. One can work to inform them, as the SPONG does, but these organizations are too jealous of their independence and autonomy. One can't even coordinate them at the national level. It is more difficult to carry out social and development projects. So, what will the international forum really do? At and after the Dakar meeting, however, the Director seemed much more optimistic about the prospects for a strong and effective African VDO movement.

CASE STUDY THREE -- MALI

I. Introduction

As a Sahelian country hard hit by drought twice in a little more than a decade, Mali is very familiar with a large number of external and a growing number of indigenous nongovernmental relief agencies. Nonetheless, many of the approximately 130 such organizations operating there have come recently. Both the older and the newer organizations have diversified their activities well beyond relief into a variety of development projects.

Mali can be considered to be entering a third phase of its relationship with the bulk of the VDO community. First, at the beginning of the 1980s drought and with the influx of organizations, a free-for-all atmosphere prevailed and there were virtually no guidelines. Then, in 1984, efforts were made to take things in charge, and structures of authorisation, reporting and control were established on both sides. Various meetings were held among and between the communities involved (government, donors, VDOs). This coincided with the inauguration of the whole "initiative de base" approach, which sought to achieve greater integration among all the actors in development all along the line between the central ministries and the local villages, and was aimed as much at the ministries themselves, as at the VDOs. Now, as we enter the third phase, there is pending serious tightening of procedures.

Among many government officials, a stimulus for VDO location in Mali is thought to be not simply severity of drought-related problems, but the revolution in Burkina Faso. Following that revolution many organizations are thought to have relocated to Mali and elsewhere. It is generally admitted by government and VDO leadership alike that until very recently, Mali provided a very open and permissive framework within which these organizations could work. The Mali Government was happy to receive them and assist them. They were coming at a time of crisis, with supplies, money, and other resources. However, the Government did not know precisely how many there were, or what resources they were bringing. Some established themselves without even having to get formal approval to operate there.

Even after a decade of experience with some of the VDOs, some of the relevant government bureaus believe that Mali still provides an unusually permissive environment for external VDOs. They increasingly question if the VDO phenomenon will be a "flash in the pan". Can it be relied on to continue to provide needed resources? Will NGO/ VDO personnel really offer specialized skills? Some government people seemed convinced that external NGOs are essentially "transferring" unemployment from the industrial countries to their own. A growing number of local university graduates are unemployed, while the VDOs bring in people with entry-level credentials, who, it is thought, couldn't find work at home of comparable responsibility, or who are merely seeking to avoid military obligations, etc..

Now, in the third phase, the atmosphere is changing in Mali. The days of "free wheeling" are limited. Mechanisms for closer control, reporting, coordinated planning and action are being put into place. At the same time, however, some promising institutional innovations are being designed that may enhance the freedom and scope of VDO activity.

II. Perceptions by Mali VDO Leaders

A. VDO Perceptions about the Actors: People and Products

    1. Indigenous Organizations:

        a. The Federation of VDOs -- C.C.A.

The VDO community is coming to be rather well organized in Mali through what was initially (January 1984) a Government-inspired committee to coordinate food relief efforts. It operates autonomously, with some external funding, and sixty-six members -- about half of the VDOs registered to operate in the country. It appears that about twelve of the CCA members are indigenous organizations. Now named The "Comité de Coordination des Actions des Organizations Non Gouvernementales" (CCA-ONG, hereafter CCA) it holds weekly planning and reporting meetings, has done some project identification, sent missions abroad to search for support, does some monitoring of projects, has a substantial project to document the work of the VDOs, organizes annual conferences between the government and the VDO community, and even acts as a disbursement agency for some external funders.

Their dues are 50,000 CFA a year for each member organization, which brings them 6 to 7 million CFA. The rest comes from PACT (2m), Oxfam-America (6m) and Live Aid/Band Aid, as well as fund-raising activities. The total annual budget is 24m. CFA. It has a staff of 16 people, of which one is expatriate, and a seven-member Board, of which two are representatives of indigenous VDOs.

The CAA publishes a periodic mimeographed bulletin, *L'Info-Hebdo*, about its own activities, those of the VDOs, and important developments in government or society relating to their work. An annual directory on the CAA members is published, [43] using a computerized data base covering the characteristics and basic descriptive information of the organizations and their activities. The directory categories the organizations by type of activity, location of projects, and nationality and affiliations, organizational characteristics. It also gives information about potential external funding and support sources.

Despite all these publications, meetings, conferences and information bases, however, there is relatively little written material available on the VDO experience in Mali. An important background paper was written for the visit of Mrs. Mitterand in 1986 which attempted to identify the problems being confronted by the VDOs.

Both for the CCA itself, and the member organizations, the CCA leadership stresses the continuing need for external subsidies. They hold up as a model of external assistance the Canadian official aid program which devotes 50% of its funds for "micro-realisations" projects of the VDOs. They found positive and negative features to their relationships with Live Aid/ Band Aid and the USAFA, discussed later in this report.

b. Groupe des Jeunes: An important, innovative development in Mali, as in Niger, has been the organization of young, otherwise unemployed university graduates into an organization that contracts with the CCA to carry out field evaluation and project monitoring activities. They produce the publications for CCA and do a number of specialized studies for the organization. They seem not yet to have established an organization for direct project implementation, although there are indigenous VDOs led and staffed by local, young, university graduates, but these tend to be affiliated with external funding sources.

c. Other indigenous VDOs. The OAMES (Oeuvre Maliènne d'Aide à l'Enfance du Sahel) is a good example of an able, indigenous organization with direct project implementation. It is not clear whether it has individual members. A General Assembly, meeting annually, elects a 7 member Administrative Bureau which, with three technical assistants, meets monthly. There is a staff of four persons, and local committees in the two regions of the country where they have project activity.

---

[43] G.A.P. publication, *Allo, Les ONG?, Annuaire 1986.*

The OAMES leader was the only Malian to serve on the selection committee that screened project proposals for funding by the USAFA (see Below.) This person has also played a role in assisting and promoting other local organizations. His assessment of these organizations is therefore important. He found weaknesses in a number of the indigenous groups and especially in their formulation of projects. They need training in how to formulate and present project proposals. They also confront problems in providing proposals in any other language than French. Thus, these groups tended to fare badly in the funding process, something unfortunate and unnecessary.

Some of the indigenous organizations are quite experienced. Many are working in neglected regions of the country. With appropriate help they can do a good job in elaborating the ideals and felt needs of villagers into project activity. The OAMES itself claims to place responsibility for the work on the village people, bringing them help in purchasing, accounting, and finding or providing the funding, doing monitoring, evaluation and reporting. Their organization works in primary health care in a frontier arrondissement, has some small projects providing stores and work for displaced herders, and has projects to stabilize and localize migrant populations coming into the larger towns. Some of these activities are carried out in association with other indigenous groups.

They receive funding from World Education in Boston, and are the local agents for a promising innovative, umbrella funding arrangement with the Canadian aid agency. In an "action de concertation" with the Canadian CIDA, they run a "Delegate Fund" that operates with a three person management committee to allocate funds to indigenous VDOs. The fund has a commitment of 34m CFA (about $100,000) and includes funds for the central administrative costs of sponsoring groups.

2. Expatriate organizations:

Of the approximately 55 members of the CCA that are of external origin, less than half were created before the 1970s, and only two located in Mali before the drought of the early 1970s. At least 32 came to Mali only during the 1980s. There has therefore been an appreciable recent proliferation of external agencies operating in the country.

All the VDOs, local or expatriate, of course, have to work within the framework of local authority and laws. But, despite the relatively lax official framework, the external VDOs have tended to ask for greater control over their efforts in health and relief work, especially. The expatriate organizations pride themselves on managerial capability, and believe that this is crucial to continued external donor largess. Sustainability of their projects also depends on the managerial dimension, which is the distinctively difficult aspect of their work. The expatriate VDO leadership sometimes expressed the belief that the Government feels it already has substantial managerial capability available. Some of the organizations are now contemplating hiring more local personnel and cutting back on their expatriate staff. AFRICARE, for example, asserted that nationals run their projects, and that "the way to go in the future is to have them better represented on the central staff as well."

Some of the expatriate organizations, although authorized to operate throughout the country, have chosen to limit themselves to certain sectors and regions, in order to perform better. They tend to think of their operations as pilot programs of some sort that later would be duplicated on a grander scale by themselves and others, including the government. An example is the Save the Children Foundation (SCF), which did not come to Mali to do emergency relief, although they did try to contribute in that sector, but rather conceives of itself in Mali as specialized in health. They stress longer term development work in the health sector. The SCF is not alone in proclaiming a philosophy of working themselves out of a job and turning their operations over to locals but neither they nor anyone else has yet done so at a level any higher than that of an individual local project, or could articulate a formula or model whereby indigenization of the regional or central operations would occur.

3. Government Institutions, as Perceived by VDO Leadership:

Some of the leadership of the VDO community, especially among the expatriate groups, believe that, following the proliferation of VDOs, the government has become more organized and demanding. The government is thought to be preoccupied with the major international and bi-lateral donors, and not yet to have a handle on the VDO situation. The government is proceeding with prudence, but without great effort, according to our interviews, with a focus on getting reports.

The general set-up is divided between administration and the technical ministries. The Ministries of Foreign Affairs and/or Interior, with which the organizations first register, now quickly pass them on to the relevant technical ministry, such as Social Affairs, Agriculture, Elevage, Health, etc.. This fits within the new policy of governmental decentralization. Administrative contacts involve the lower departmental levels of government, at the region, cercle, arrondissement, and the like.

The functioning of the machinery to handle emergency relief is thought to reflect the more general picture. The "Comité National d'Aide aux Victimes de la Secheresse" (CNAVS) handles the distribution of cereals. It has thirty-five members, including donors, governments, and individual VDOs as well as the CCA. The committee has received aid from external donors, such as USAID, and the UNDP, to help with transportation aspects. They handled $10m worth of relief supplies in 1984/5 and $50m (including the assistance for transport) in 85/6 but will soon run out of funds. VDOs were used to distribute some (about 35,000 tons) of the assistance in the early 1987 round. The Committee really runs a rather autonomous operation, however, with its own secretariat, but with government not yet granting it separate status. Some cereal distribution is thought to have gone through the Ministry directly, and was badly distributed. The Ministry departments still rather tightly control the allocation system, to the extent that they can.

B. VDO Perceptions about Spacial Location of Activities:

The VDOs do tend to concentrate in sectors and regions. Their leadership did not raise this as a problem however. Indeed, the leadership of one very prominent and active organization thought that it might be advantageous -- promoting cooperation with others, although the organizations also do tend to bump into each other, and there could be some overlap. They acknowledge that the government wants, with good reasons, a more even spread of activity around the country. One important VDO leader questioned the expectation that VDOs should work in areas that the GOM is unwilling to support.

Some thought that political processes tend to help counterbalance the concentration, because active and concerned representatives from remote regions have been able to attract support, and to get the government to push programs in their areas. Strong local leadership or Deputies to the National Assembly have been able to attract organizations, such as AFRICARE, into regions not in its original plans, or even within the scope of the Country Development Strategy Statement of its funding source, the USAID.

The SCF mentioned its pilot Extended Program of Immunizations, (EPI) project in the Fifth Region (Mpoti) of Mali, which they worked out with the Ministry of Health, but which is now, by their own choice, the only place in the country where they work. Other organizations have shifted regions to avoid duplication. "Medicins sans Frontiers", for example, moved to the sixth region (Timbuktu), Croix de Malta the seventh (Gao), OMS-CMI in the Cercle Badio etc. Primary health care is concentrated in the fourth region (Segu). All these arrangements were worked out with the Ministry, but it lacks funds and some of SCF's efforts elsewhere will collapse. Points of connection with the national strategy are always taken into account, but the lack of government funding halts some efforts in places.

C. VDO Perceptions about Procedures:

1. Registration/Authorization:

There are three tiers of administration to go through: national, regional and local. VDOs have to be authorized at each level, to fit into the Development Plan operations there, and have to keep in contact with authorities. No VDO leader cited the procedures of getting a protocol or general authorisation to operate in the country as a problem. Approvals for visits and/or operations at the more local levels could be a problem, but this aspect, also, was not emphasized in the discussions with VDO leaders. [44]

2. Communications:

How the organizations get along with the administration depends on personality, style of operation, and diligence in touching base early on. If the national leadership knows the operation, one can get along OK, the VDO leadership thinks, but one needs to spend a minimum amount of time "courting" the national figures and regional administrators. avoidance of whom can cause serious constraints. Perseverance counts considerably in one's success. The ministers and governmental officials do not see much of the projects, and although the VDOs give their annual reports, little attention is paid to these. One experienced organization thought that only the Ministry of Plan has really asked for reports. Another person, from a bi-lateral donor, thought that the Ministry of Foreign Affairs (MFA) used to have a person responsible for the VDOs, who standardized the protocol, but had left and not been replaced [This is most likely an official in the Ministry of Territorial Administration (MTA) he had in mind, and is erroneous in as much as the official was replaced]. There is not yet even a full contingent of ministers, and no one is charged with the responsibility to follow the VDO activities.

The government does have clear guidelines for authorization, and all the key ministries are involved, but there is still lack of leadership and direction. This may tempt VDOs to attempt to work on their own, but informed observers in the international organization community are convinced that VDOs can accomplish much more working through the governmental machinery.   The government wants development plans and emergency

---

[44] One VDO leader subsequently noted that the GOM was known to be reviewing the entire protocol process.

distribution plans, and wants the organizations to connect well with the local administration, especially the commandant de cercle.

The meetings the VDO leadership has had with government officials, however, have tended to be long and chaotic.

3. Taxes and Duties:

VDO leadership is convinced that the government is tightening controls. They feel the are now going to be taxed, despite the development contributions they bring into the country. One VDO leader subsequently asserted that the GOM often puts the VDOs in a "catch 22 situation" in as much as the delays they cause in the granting of the tax exemptions occasions large storage charges.

4. Freedom for VDO Activity:

Some of the prominent VDO leaders feel that the government has a problem with the idea of VDO activity, especially with the philosophy of independence that the VDOs are thought to embody.

5. Funding:

Some of the VDO leadership expressed the belief that the GOM had run out of money, and so its machinery concerned with VDOs was not functioning. The emergency assistance funds were also about depleted, although there   still was some funding available for cereal distribution, including its transportation. It was not clear there would be a continuing need for this assistance, but very it was evident that government revenues were severely limited.

The CAA leadership was also concerned to have the external funders to the VDOs schedule the release of funds to the local organizations. They believe that the CAA itself offers a good route for a controlled and timely distribution of funds to VDOs. One leader of an external VDO noted, however, that the rather sophisticated fund-raising techniques of some of the VDOs allow them to remain autonomous from government funding sources, but even for some of these, and certainly for those receiving government support, it is important that their headquarters remain in control over funds. "Unfortunately, most of the monies obtained by PVOs for development projects overseas are not for them to do with as they please. PVO's are held directly accountable by their donors who have confidence in their (the PVO's) managerial capabilities," he stated. "The PVO's often must jump through endless hoops and adhere to countless regulations to be granted

USAID monies. The point here is that the CCA, like the Malian Government, is not fully aware of the politics behind PVO donor assistance and is under an illusion if they think that PVO's are going to funnel donor constituency funds through them." He also noted that the available funding is affected by a great many things, including the general condition of the economy in the source country, effective use of the media, the activities of particular interest groups, in addition to occurrence of natural disaster. In other words, availability of substantial funding is not assured.

VDO leaders knew that the there was emerging a new approach to channeling external funds, through a "Cellule d'appui aux Initiatives de Base". The Germans have put up some of the funding for this, and the government is trying to regroup the donors, especially those that channel their funds through the VDOs.

6. Fit with the Plan:

The VDOs do feel they are included in the planning machinery and reflected in the national development strategy. Some of the VDOs, in health for example, believe that their activity preceded the Plan, and they note that, in any case, the GOM budget has not favored the health sector, which has consistently received less than 8% of GNP. Scarcity of resources obviously constrains attention to preventive care, unless the elite decides on clear priorities for such, within a comprehensive planning process. That, however, is lacking.

The Mali approach to an extended program of immunization (EPI), or its commitment to primary health care, was not constructed anticipating the VDOs coming in, but VDOs are important in it now, and their commitments are holding up. The individual VDOs had to negotiate separately with the government. The most recent to arrive was UNICEF itself, which has provided $5m for the five-year EPI, for example. However, these funds may be too limited to do the job.

The national strategy had been to do the EPI without help, and to have vaccines at the local medical centers, with supervision and training teams at the regional level. The national strategy has been modified a bit, because the government didn't initially expect to be able to have national coverage, but to have a system in place after five years. This is now accelerated. However, there still is no indication how recurrent costs are going to be covered, although there are some recipient fees. There is a regional cold-chain for the immunizations, and some of the VDOs have their own. Essentially, the SCF has adopted the Mali national strategy, rather than the other way around, although it was involved in the planning.

On food aid, the VDO leadership believes that the government is concerned about price distortions in the market for local foods. The VDOs participate on the committee that supervises such distributions. The country as a whole was thought to have decent grain reserves.

D. VDO Perceptions about the Major Problems:

1. Tax and Import Duty Exemptions: This topic was not raised by the VDO leadership, as an existing problem. See Section C.3 above for more on this topic.

2. Government Appreciation of and Attention to VDOs:

VDO leadership tend to think the government is not very appreciative of their efforts. They think the governmental officials know little of their activity, and will not go to look. Some feel there are no local criteria for evaluating VDO action in the field. The government doesn't realize that the requirements to connect with so many layers of local administration entails what the VDOs think is a large waste of their resources.

VDO leaders tend to think that their organizations are efficient conveyers of resources directly to local producers, whereas very little of the governments' resources every "trickle down" to the peasants in developing countries. They also feel that they have to give a good account of the use of their funds, where governments do not.

The VDOs think they did a great job responding to the food crisis in Mali, given the pressure they were under. Some of them feel that they never got much in the way of "thanks" for their efforts. Although one VDO leader cautioned that the VDO record was good in light of their inexperience in Mali, another pointed out that the principal distributors of food aid here, The Baptist Mission, World Vision, and CARE, are among the most experienced in food relief work around the world.

3. Special Funding Program

a. U.S.A. for Africa: Indigenous organizations did not fare well in the first round of funding. They were disadvantaged. They have little experience or expertise in drafting proposals, and no means to translate them into English. Some of the indigenous organizations felt that the news had not gotten around sufficiently. On the second funding round, where the Request for Proposals mentioned a special concern to fund indigenous organizations, they were encourage and assisted.

       b. Training: One of the organizations giving help to the indigenous groups stressed that local groups need training in proposal preparation and presentation.

4. Other Special Problems:

One problem cited by an important external VDO leader was the need to get the GOM functionaries out of their offices in Bamako and into the field. There are a number of committed, skillful and experienced people among them, yet the lack of resources limits their contribution. "They have the skills but are destined to baby-sit floundering programs due to the lack of funds," he stated, and questioned, "What is the answer?"

The displacement of people from drought areas was also stressed as a continuing problem, requiring stepped-up intervention. One example of programs to relate to this issue is the Oxfam-America program to assist resettled Dogon villagers in the South of the country. In a program that started with twelve families, in a new self-built village, the Dogon settlers have been assisted to acquire farming equipment (cows, donkeys, carts, ploughs). Farmers are given loans to purchase these items, and other VDO programs are used in tandem to manufacture some of the purchased material. The project is expanding slowly in order to establish a pattern of loan repayment. Yet new settlers, family members of those already there, are continuing to come in, straining the capacity of the village. It is not clear to anyone involved how they can resolve the problem of continued expansion.

III. MALI GOVERNMENT AND INTERNATIONAL AGENCY OFFICIAL PERCEPTIONS

General Introduction:

In general, government officials concerned with the VDO sector say that the government is oriented toward changing its pattern of development administration, and thus of relating to the VDOs, to add a local level integrated-development type program similar to Niger or Burkina Faso. The professed intent is to transfer the competence for development promotion to the population itself. The authorities at the most local level are not paid by the state (Chef de village, Conseil de Village) but should be the real planners. Little by little, government officials say, they will be charged with real responsibility over all matters that really affect their interests and touch their lives.

Some officials concerned with this process, somewhat oddly, question whether it is right or appropriate for external aid to come into these operations through VDOs. They do not profess to be sure of the answer. They say they must assess the impact these organizations have had. The system, with the new "initiative de base" aspect, is now complicated, but doesn't have to be. They are concerned to make it work with greater coherence. One official predicted, however, that within two years or so, external VDOs would no longer be involved.

A. Govt. Perceptions on the Actions: People/ Products:

1. Indigenous Organizations: Not much was said among the government officials about the indigenous groups. They seem to regard such groups as externally affiliated. The CCA itself is known, and the annual conferences, the "journee de reflexion" are also visible.

Relevant Government officials defined VDOs (they used the former terminology of NGO) as non-profit organizations working at the grass-roots to give food aid or health assistance, and the like.

2. Expatriate: Several officials expressed concern about the proliferation of organizations and wondered if they would bring longer term commitments. The VDOs in the health field are thought by the Ministry to have provided an enormously important input into health, public hygiene and social action. Territorial administration was aware of about twenty organizations that had played a role in providing relief supplies.

Government officials expressed anger at perceived VDO accusations that the government wanted to dominate and suppress its own population. There is recognized good will on the part of many, perhaps most VDOs, but there is a sense that a crisis is underway or pending.

An official thought the crisis concerned especially the CAA, some American organizations, and perhaps the Canadian aid program because of the latter's refusal to participate in the "Cellule d'Appui aux Initiatives de Base" (yet, the Canadians have gone the furthest in supporting indigenous VDOs, and the CAA expressed a clear preference for that model.)

The volunteer corps, such as the Peace Corps, were also criticized as bringing young people more concerned with fitting into the local community, and maintaining good relations there, than in really doing what may be necessary to achieve progress and resolve problems, so they don't really hold the local people accountable. Yet, government officials also sometimes named the Peace Corps volunteers as the best performers.

Some of the VDO leaders that participated in the "Journee de Reflexion" conference were thought to be overly rigid in their positions, becoming a prisoner of them.

3. Government Institutions:

Given the lack of staff, funding, or other means for the government to follow up with VDOs, and the practical non- functioning of the Commission Nationale de Suivi in the Ministry of Territorial Administration, which has had no means to get out into the field where the activities occur, an institutional reorganization is being contemplated.

The new program of "développement intégral de la base" instituted in June of 1986, is supposed to involve tightly coordinated and integrated planning and follow-up by all the relevant and concerned ministries at the local level. The chef and Conseil de Village would be the authoritative body at the most local level. "Secteurs de développement" would group six to twelve villages having similar situations. At the arrondissement level there will be a Council that will group representatives from all the concerned ministries for any given project or program. It is this council that will have to approve any new project. Some of the VDO leaders expressed the belief that this will turn out to be a highly politicized process.

Local village level representatives will have to explain their objectives. Plans will be harmonized at the level of the Cercle, one step higher. Then as these plans go up to the region and the national level, they would rarely be changed in any major way. There are elected structures at each of these levels, to approve the programs worked out by the technical committees at that level.

The officials involved believe that, little by little, these structures will transfer real power and responsibility to the people. It is not clear how VDOs would fit into that picture, although no one suggested they could not. We should note that some of the VDO leadership expressed the belief that this whole initiative will prove to be a sham that was meant to quiet the peasants.

B. Perceptions about Spacial Location:

Government is generally critical of the distribution pattern of VDO activity. Official policy is designed to achieve a better distribution of operations and to favor those groups willing to act accordingly, preventing others who simply duplicate the actions already going on. It is felt that some VDOs only want to work where they can be highly visible; that few want to work where it is difficult or remote. (Note that this is in sharp contrast to the self image of the VDOs themselves, although one important external VDO leader expressed the opinion that VDOs should not be expected to work in areas that the GOM itself was unwilling to support.)

Some American groups were singled out for criticism by the Ministry of Plan, with regard to poorly choosing its zones, and not wanting to go where there were no other external groups.

C. Government perceptions about Procedures:

1. Registration/Authorization:

Prior to 1984, VDOs operated on the basis of a "work agreement" negotiated with the Ministry of Foreign Affairs and the National Direction for International Cooperation. Since late 1984 the present procedures for authorization have been in place, and start with The Ministry of Territorial Administration, which requires a copy of three things: a) legal statutes of the organization; b) the composition of the governing board; and c) who their representative is in Mali. They claim to be interested only to know that the organization is led by people of high moral standing. (They might even have their own embassy check out the organization in the country/people of origin.) The only criteria is that the organization be non-profit and have an humanitarian orientation, with emergency aid, development assistance or the like, and have financing.

If all is well, a standardized basic accord is signed (an "Accord typique") by Interior, and a Protocol of Agreement issued by the Ministry of the Plan. This document is specific about where in the country and in what activity the organization may operate. In principle, it also indicates the financing to be provided for the year. Then other specialized ministries may also be required to grant approval, in an "Accord particulier".

2. Communication:

Government officials say the VDOs must take the national plan into account, at every level, and respect the government's approach to development. They must also report on their activities each three months, as that is how often the Comité de Développement and the other technical ministries report to the Ministry of Plan. There is also the annual meeting between the government and all the VDOs in development. The government does not hide its desire to channel the action of the VDOs, to achieve coordinated and harmonized action.

In September of 1985 there was an important Journee de Reflexion which brought the major VDOs together with the concerned ministries. Each side expressed its pent up gripes. Participants claim that it was not easy going at the beginning. Government people feel, still, that there was a spirit of suspicion and scorn toward them by the VDOs. They have now had four such annual meetings and the atmosphere has cleared quite a bit.

But problems remain regarding reporting , evaluation and follow up. It is felt that local level structures are sending in their reports, but that not all the VDOs provide theirs. The Ministry of Territorial Administration was to have a Bureau de Suivi, but had no means to really follow up. They claim that the required reports are not coming in, and the bureau feels that it cannot keep up with the field activities of the 129 registered organizations. There remain many obstacles, including lack of means for villages to elaborate projects.

There is the feeling that the time has arrived to get a good idea of what the contribution of the VDO sector is. (See more on this issue in the discussion of "Plan Fit" below.)

3. Taxes and duties: No government official mentioned any problem in this area.

4. Freedom for the VDOs: Government, especially Territorial Administration, claimed that they want to leave the VDOs free and that they do value the VDO contributions.

5. Funding: Some of the experienced government officials who have worked with the VDOs question whether it is right for external development assistance to come so much in this form. They also wonder how Malian organizations can get direct funding from abroad.

It is felt that too much of the original financing for the VDOs goes into their own administrative costs. One official with responsibilities in this sector estimated that only about 5% of the receipts of the VDOs abroad wind up being put directly into development assistance on the ground. They question even the CAA, with its 20m CFA budget and three vehicles, when the responsible governmental bureaus have no means to do field reviews.

6. Plan Fit:

That VDO activity should fit into the overall development plan and the country's approach is a given. We have no evidence that any VDO in Mali seriously rejects the Plan priorities etc., yet we think they would be surprised by the conviction held by certain important governmental officials that VDOs have not fit into the plan structure very well.

There is widespread governmental concern to channel the VDO, to have them go to where activity is lacking, where the government itself is weak, so as to redress imbalances. They wanted, also, to have VDOs take on some of the projects that had been pressed on the government from local groups, or even from strong political figures, where it seemed appropriate. These were aims of the "initiative de base" program and have been in place for some time. They feel, however, that neither all the donors (who expressed some support for this approach) nor the VDOs have given sufficient support to the scheme.

Now, in preparations for the next five year plan, one in which the government anticipates and hopes for a large role for the VDOs, an assessment is being made of the five years or so of experience with a multitude of VDOs. A National Committee for Evaluation of NGOs, presided over by the Minister of Plan, and including the Minister of Foreign Affairs and of Interior, with a secretariat and involving a number of relevant subordinate officials, has been evaluating the experience. The complaints are the same as before -- a need to adapt to the priorities, to achieve a more even spread, longer term commitments of funds, integration of the VDO activities with local and middle level Plan formulations.

The structures are there and clear, from the village level, where there is a Chef and Conseil de village, up through the arrondissement, cercle, region, each with an elected Conseil that must approve of the overall plan for that level, and a technical Comité de Développement that integrates the projects and interventions of the technical ministries, each of which must approve the projects and work of the VDOs and anyone else involved.

Experience in the health field was cited as an example of both positive and negative results. The work of the VDOs in Segou was singled out as a good model, where careful integration with the various plans was achieved. But elsewhere there were problems, such as organizations wanting to put in a hospital at the village level when GOM policy requires hospitals to serve many villages, or VDOs wanting to use para-medics or assistants to do vaccinations.

The Ministry complained that whereas their program now focusses on six specific common children illnesses (measles, DPT etc.) some of the groups wanted to work on AIDS. In some of the rural health programs VDOs were bringing in drugs with different dosages than their people were used to. The training programs at the local level foreseen in the Plan are to cover specific content. The Ministry demands that these actions and interventions be rationalized and coordinated.

There is also, now, the emergence of a new approach to channeling funding to the VDOs, being formulated in a program of Cellule d'appui des Initiatives de base. (This is discussed below under Prospects.)

3: Special Funding Programs:-- United Support of Artists for Africa (USAFA):

Government and international donor agency personnel were certainly aware of the funding provided by this organization and some of the issues that emerged in connection with its support for work in Mali. The officials we interviewed thought (correctly) that the CCA and AFRICARE were the principal sources of leadership in organizing the VDO community to prioritize its proposals for funding from this group. The USAFA had hoped to stimulate cooperation and communication among the VDOs, both expatriate and indigenous, and to have their field-based experience be the principal factor in allocating $1.5 million available to Mali in the first round of recovery and development project funding by them.

After an initial meeting of VDOs in Mali to communicate the prospects of funding and the criteria established (that favored grass-roots work in agriculture, water resources, health, etc.) a "Selection Committee" was created to go through the sixty-five or so proposals that ultimately (after a very slow start) were submitted. In addition to the CCA staff, one indigenous VDO was represented, along with AFRICARE and CARE-MALI, and the UNDP. The committee found it rather difficult to actually evaluate the proposals in order of their merit. Rather, they acted as a vetting agency, screening out those that did not fit the criteria such as rejecting those submitted in French -- a mistaken criteria established for the first cycle that was eliminated from the second cycle of USAFA funding) or were from groups with no staff or experience. A result, however, was the exclusion of a number of indigenous groups. This later led the USAFA to give emphasis to indigenous organizations in its funding orientation.

Another problem with this operation was that the funding arrived very late for some groups, and in one case, not soon enough to start the project (that group had to find funding elsewhere). Communications with the USAFA headquarters were very poor.

D. Government Perceptions of Problems:

1. Tax and Duties: no mention was made of any problem in this domain.

2. Government attention to and appreciation of the VDOs: The officials generally mixed their criticisms with an assertion that they do appreciate the good-will and resourceful contributions of the VDOs.

3. Special Funding Programs -- United Support of Artists for Africa (USAFA):

Government and international donor agency personnel were certainly aware of the funding provided by this organization and some of the issues that emerged in connection with its support for work in Mali. The officials we interviewed thought (correctly) that the CCA and AFRICARE were the principal sources of leadership in organizing the VDO community to prioritize its proposals for funding from this group. The USAFA had hoped to stimulate cooperation and communication among the VDOs, both expatriate and indigenous, and to have their field-based experience be the principal factor in allocating $1.5 million available to Mali in the first round of recovery and development project funding by them.

After an initial meeting of VDOs in Mali to communicate the prospects of funding and the criteria established (that favored grass-roots work in agriculture, water resources, health, etc.) a "Selection Committee" was created to go through the sixty-five or so proposals that ultimately (after a very slow start) were submitted. In addition to the CCA staff, one indigenous VDO was represented, along with AFRICARE and CARE-MALI, and the UNDP. The committee found it rather difficult to actually evaluate the proposals in order of their merit. Rather, they acted as a vetting agency, screening out those that did not fit the criteria such as those submitted in French -- a mistaken criteria established for the first cycle that was eliminated from the second cycle of USAFA funding -- or that were from groups with no staff or experience. A result, however, was the exclusion of a number of indigenous groups. This later led the USAFA to give emphasis to indigenous organizations in its funding orientation.

Another problem with this operation was that the funding arrived very late for some groups, and in one case, not soon enough to start the project (that group had to find funding elsewhere). Communications with the USAFA headquarters were very poor.

4. Other Problems: Use of Local Youth

A surprising number of high placed government officials have expressed the view that VDOs are essentially transferring unemployment from the home industrial country to Mali. In this assertion they repeated exactly arguments advanced by some Niger government officials. However rhetorical, or aimed at political effect the assessment may be, it is probably nurtured by concern about the growing number of unemployed Malian university graduates, in the midst of substantial VDO activity that utilizes young expatriate personnel with no more substantial education. The Malians believe that many of these volunteers would not have jobs at home of comparable responsibility, or may be seeking to avoid military service. "Those who come do not know anything about Africa," one high official asserted. He thinks that they often wind up in "vice" in Mali.

A more widespread concern is to have the expatriate organizations actually accomplish a transfer of skills and competencies. They should limit themselves to two or three expatriates, who are really specialists, and work with indigenous people to train them. These organizations should make use of our own "diplomés" one official argued, who have now have an organization of their own (the "groupe des jeunnes") with a permanent staff. "We want to see them used, instead of the NGO importing in their own staff from the exterior." And, they add, if they do use the local people, this should lead to a transfer of capacity to continue the work, not only at the project level, but at the level of the sponsoring organization as well. The technical assistance aspect should disappear over time. Right now, they think, even at the level of the projects, very little transfer of competence is occurring. "This is not going to be allowed to continue" pledged one official.

So far, the expatriate VDO community has given its support to the CCA whose Malian staff does represent them before the various organs of government. The CCA also has engaged the "groupe des jeunes" to do some of its studies and field monitoring. However, this group has not yet been able to present itself as an VDO with direct field project programs for external funding.

E. Government Perception of Prospects

1. General funding patterns: Government personnel are fearful that a shift in funding patterns may be underway, from the type of bi-lateral and multi-lateral support that has for so long assisted the governmental programs, to the VDOs. Already, they claim, the VDOs have influenced the donors to shift toward small project actions. There donors, they think, seem to prefer to give a little here and a little there, through "fly-by-night" operations, rather

than a large sum that the national government could manage. [45] The VDOs they support now come with only short-term funding, unable to say if they have funding for successive years, and with no long-term planning. This disturbs the government officials.

2.   Government personnel had no direct comments to make about umbrella funding, or grants to local on-granting facilities, except to say that they had something of a crisis with the Canadians, who were refusing to give support to the new Initiative de Base program, even though they were committed to support "micro-realisations".

It is curious that the Initiative de Base program was interpreted by the Canadians to be in competition with a micro-realisations approach. They have supported just such a program elsewhere (in Niger, for example) and are among the most ready to support indigenous VDO activity. They may have wanted to await clarification of the role in the scheme the VDOs would play. It may also be that the new program, discussed next, was devised to answer concerns such as those seemingly held by the Canadians.

3.   "Cellule d'appui des Initiatives de Base"

This represents a new institutional arrangement which was just being worked out during our visit to Mali. It could hold promise not only for a larger role in development for VDOs but their more direct involvement in on-granting decisions for allocating funds to this sector.

This effort seems to reflect the convergence of several streams of activity and concern: 1) the government's concern to redynamize its "Commission de Suivi des ONG" which was in the Ministry of Territorial Administration, and charged with monitoring the VDOs but lacked funding; 2) the government's concern to achieve greater planing and operational coherence in development activity at the local level; 3) the interests of certain donors to promote VDO and small scale local projects; and 4) the VDOs' interest in playing a more direct role in funding decisions and planning processes.

Funding pledges have come from the Germans, the EEC, the UNDP, Belgians, and others. It will involve a new structure outside the ministries,

---

[45]. Note that many specialists now assert the need for an "alternative model of development" that would directly support local level activity. Given the perception of wide- spread governmental failures, corruption, and inefficiency, they argue that large sums for development assistance should not go through the governments.

the Donors Round-table and the CCA (as the federation of the NGOs) that will have para-statal status from the government. The Ministry of Territorial Administration and the Ministry of Planning, both of which have participated in the elaboration of the cellule, will be represented on it. The CCA has also attended the planning meetings that had been held by the time of our visit in May, 1987.

As foreseen at that time, (the plans were not complete, and certainly had not yet received Governmental approval) the VDOs would execute 60% - 70% of the projects. Certain of the major donors evidently thought it would mean their losing control of funding decision-making. The UNDP felt that, on the contrary, this would bring together the donors and regroup them for more effective participation. It would also rationalize and make more efficient the government's participation. The new agency would combine all the activities concerned with small scale project promotion -- from financing and contracting, to monitoring and evaluation. The government and the VDOs would wind up working closer to the donors. They hope it will make clear the rules and criteria to everybody. There is some confusion in the discussion of the project, however. Some officials in the Ministry of Plan think that the new Cellule would not monitor all of the VDO activity, or even all of the "initiatives de base".

A concomitant aspect of this development is the codification and integration of all the legal texts and regulations bearing on the development promotion process. A Conseil d'Administration, again, presided over by the Minister of Territorial Administration, is in the process of uniting all of the national policy and financing texts. Part of the aim is to enhance the program of decentralization, leading to greater autonomy of the regions, each of which will take charge of itself in these domains.

The participation in the discussions of the VDO community through the CCA is important, although somewhat controversial. In the early phases of the discussion it seems that the CCA made a poorly conceived bid to implement the whole program. Some of the donors felt that the CCA was not up to the job, and others felt they could be able to play a key role with more training. One major bi-lateral donor pushed for a very large role for VDOs but was not in favor of the CCA being the key agency itself. Yet it seems clear that they will be involved in some of the decision making, and could come to play a key role in the monitoring and evaluation process. The government has been most concerned that there be a robust evaluation and monitoring process and feels that it was the donors who resisted this, perhaps out of fear of government stifling the local activity. It seems that, at the moment, about $.5m is pledged to the process, a level of activity the VDOs could handle.

CASE STUDY FOUR -- GHANA

I. Introduction:

Use of private-sector organizations devoted to promotion of development on the basis of volunteer contributions or non-profit activity is a well-established tradition in Ghana. Almost every village has some such organization at work, usually created by the more successful of its sons or daughters. Additionally, there are many such organizations that may work on a broader basis, that may have been inspired by religious movements or churches, or by previous political parties or government.

There is no comprehensive directory of such organizations, although the Catholic Relief Services (CRS) in Ghana has completed (although not yet issued) a very useful guide to the larger or more significant ones. Presently, the central federation of VDOs in Ghana, the Ghana Association of Private Volunteer Organizations in Development (GAPVOD), is attempting to compile a complete directory, encouraged by the U.N.D.P.; the Government itself is also interested to have an inventory. Lack of communication between various interested parties is evident, however. We found scanty familiarity with the others' efforts among these various groups. GAPVOD leadership seemed unaware, for example, of the existence of the CRS directory.

The CRS directory lists 15 non-sectarian organizations and 24 that it calls church-related. The GAPVOD staff believes that there are a great many more, even excluding the hundreds if not thousands of organizations that represent collective or group efforts at improvement at the village or sub-regional level. In a national registry of organizations with social action or impact, kept by the Ministry of Social Welfare, about three hundred organizations are said to be listed.

As the GAPVOD has pointed out, although the action was often highly politicized in the service of the colonial enterprise, "missionaries and the churches they established continued to initiate and consolidate development beneficial to the mass of the people." [46]   Subsequently, the independent Government of Ghana (GOG), especially during the Nkrumah years, launched many organizations among various groups of citizens, including women, youth, farmers. Some groups reacted to increasing bureaucratization and centralization by spawning new programs of local self-help and public service. By 1963 this had led to the founding of the Christian Service Committee.

Following the emergence of military rule and the end to one-party socialist-oriented rule, local private development and community self-help efforts expanded considerably. In addition to expatriate organizations such as Operations Crossroads Africa and the U.S. Peace Corps, there emerged operations such as the Voluntary Work-camps Association of Ghana (with one of the most active programs on the continent) and the Student Social Organization, as well as many organizations among Christian, especially women's, circles.

Many of these organizations are now indigenous in their governing boards and leadership, although they may have been created by churches or religious movements initially implanted in the country from abroad during colonial times. All these organizations are involved in the whole range of activities typical of such organizations elsewhere, from training in agricultural techniques and technology and management, to direct assistance in project development and funding.

There is considerable interest in promoting VDO activity by major international donor agencies. The Ghana Government also professes a concern to involve them more in development planning and action, as it attempts to restructure the society for development from below and to empower the masses.

While there is considerable complementarity in the views of VDOs, International Organizations and the GOG about the character, problems and potentialities of VDOs, there are also evident disparities and uncertainties. Following is a summary presentation of relevant comments from leaders in each of these three communities about the actors, the problems and the prospects in VDO-Official interaction in development work in Ghana.

---

[46] Case Study, GAPVOD/GHANA I for Nairobi Crossroads Workshop, 22-28 April 1987.

II. Ghana VDO Leadership Perceptions

A.   Government People and Products -- About the Actors:

Following are brief descriptions of the leadership, organizational history and characteristics of some of the more active of the indigenous organizations, as described by the leadership and promotional material from such organizations. [47]

Indigenous Organizations

1.   GAPVOD: (Ghana Association of Volunteer Organizations in Development).   This is the main federation of VDOs in Ghana. It was created in March, 1980, out of a conference that sought to achieve greater communication and coordination among the VDOs active in Ghana.   The participants wished to "inform each other of their work, to look for areas of mutual assistance and for cooperation," to quote their brochure. It lists the following objectives: 1) to collect, share and disseminate information relevant to development, including information on Government policies and programs relating to socioeconomic problems in both rural and urban areas; 2) to develop the potential of member groups to coordinate and liaise between themselves and governmental and commercial agencies; 3) to explore and seek funding resources from local and international donors.

Their organizational development has been slow and difficult. Interviews with current leadership indicated that throughout the life of the organization it has been a one-man operation. They have had a lot of turnover in leadership, and in August 1987 they were with their fourth Executive Director. One Director who was doing a good job died a year ago. The next Executive Director was there only six months. Then they got the current Director, Mr. Sarpei, on loan from the Christian Service Committee, one of their member agencies. He is a well-qualified person who energetically promotes GAPVOD, but he will soon go abroad for further studies. GAPVOD will have to decide on a new process to advertise for a new director.

Many observers thought that previously the GAPVOD had been run as a club of professionals. Membership agencies have not really gotten involved. The current Executive Director hoped to change that, to make it a real membership organization. They do have business people in the policy making body, as Chair or Board member of member agencies, but have not

---

[47] Based on some interviews, and entries in the CRS directory which was, itself, based on reports from relevant organizations.

really tapped them, even for the GAPVOD Board. Such people could help to raise money (they do already help out in this way, but few of them have discretionary funds in their businesses to allocate, as businessmen in industrial countries often have).

a. Budget: The annual budget is 5 million Cedis. The dues are 5000 Cedis a year (the official exchange rate was about Cedis 165= $, although one could get 250+ on the parallel market). GAPVOD has some service charges, that might meet 25% of budget, in the form of training fees, for example. The organization has about 20 members. The American organization, PACT, is giving C/ 1.6m, and subscriptions bring in C/ 100,000. They have to raise the rest through local activities, and the respondent implied that they hadn't yet·done so. PACT has given some funds for the administrative budget for one year, and previously sponsored their conferences and participation in the Geneva meeting, and most recently, in Dakar.

They also have an umbrella, on-granting fund, in the form of a rural development fund (RDF), as part of the PACT C/ 1.6m support. This RDF provides 187,500 Cedis for operations, (including GAPVOD); 750,000 for general administration; 375,000 for management training; 187,500 for research and publications.

b. GAPVOD Product: Their activities include the following: 1) manpower resource development in both local and overseas training programs; 2) provision of information and documentation services through a small library, their bulletins and journals, and efforts such as compilation of a directory of VDOs, and audio-visual aids for development promotion; 3) conduct of a Development Forum; and 4) various other counselling, research and representational services.

They also held a "Development Forum" two years ago, soon after their founding. The welcome address and Chairman of the meeting was provided by one of the present Board members, Mr. Doku. One of the Government Secretaries (of Rural Development, Mr. Acqua Harrison) was the guest speaker. The GAPVOD leadership feels that this meeting "established" the organization in the eyes of the government.

The organization is also completing an inventory or directory in collaboration with the UNDP. We noted above, however, that the GAPVOD leadership were unaware that the Catholic Relief Service had already done one such a directory, although of limited scope. They recognize the definitional problem of whom to include, when to consider it definitive, what form in which to publish it. The Statistical Service Department has requested GAPVOD to do this, for Ministry of Finance and Economic Planning use in its programs with the Ministries of Local Government, Rural Development and Social Welfare, and Cooperatives. GAPVOD wants these government bureaus to have information on the VDOs.

They have already had a recent meeting with the secretariat of the Commission, and agreed in principle with them to do a Forum in September, to be entitled *Considering The Role of the Private Sector.* They will prepare a paper for the Provisional National Defense Council (PNDC) to get final approval. They want the UNDP to participate as well. GAPVOD has also had a meeting with The Ministry of Rural Development and Social Welfare that was positive.

GAPVOD leaders are working on a code of ethics for these organizations (and for the private sector generally?) which they want to be like the Investment Code. A subcommittee, composed of the AARA, World Vision, and the OIC is to develop the document.

Some of their members feel, however, that the idea of having GAPVOD be the vetting agency for other VDOs is of debatable soundness.   The respondent here may have been concerned about protecting his own agency's access to funds and authorizations, having earlier expressed the belief that GAPVOD is not broadly enough based.   GAPVOD is sending out a form to the 20 members for the inventory, and then expects to hold the Development Forum to discuss the forms and need for this information. They will invite to the forum all the known groups and those extracted from the list at the Social Welfare registry, and will also advertise in the papers.

GAPVOD categorizes VDOs in Ghana into four types: 1.   PVOs involved in Development work proper, 2.   Religious/social organizations doing some development and relief work 3. Mutual aid and self-help social welfare organizations, (some of which are informal, and others are cooperatives). 4. Village improvement and development associations.

GAPVOD attempts to include and service all these groups, even at the grass roots level, to help them to carry out their own programs and not be just agents for someone else (usually an externally-based organization). They feel that the brokers decide where VDOs will work. They feel they should rather empower the grass roots people/organizations for the latters' own development efforts.   They should empower the local organizations, the cooperatives, even the savings clubs and material aid orgnizations to do development work.

The obstacle to VDOs in Ghana achieving maturity, in the opinion of GAPVOD leaders, is not lack of money, but basically the lack of management and clarification of clear objectives and training for the organizations to design and use proper accounting and accountability systems which would then enhance their ability to get loans, and/or attract funding. GAPVOD feels that some groups have already achieved some successes along these lines. They mention the TECHNOSERVE projects with the Labadi Town Improvement Organization, which is now floating shares for a bank, with The Bank of Ghana providing 5% of the equity. TECHNOSERVE, one of GAPVOD's founding member organizations, is essentially giving the training, management, and maintenance to the farmers' groups. They also have milling operations for some farmers in Ashanti (Palm Oil). TECHNOSERVE places a person there for as long as three years. They have already gone full cycle with two projects, i.e., turning over all the operations, which takes 2-3 years. Funding has never been the real problem for TECHNOSERVE.

The GAPVOD leadership wants to organize training programs within its own organization.   None of the indigenous PVOs can now place a manager with a local group. GAPVOD wants to be able to tap the collective experience, but be a "live and let live", not a "big brother" type organization, in the process.

GAPVOD does not want to run operations in the field, and become a competitor to its own member agencies, and cites what they call "the sad example of GONGAT" (Togo) which was not only taken over by the Party, but ran competitive field operations that alienated its members. This is why GAPVOD raised this issue, seemingly successfully, at the FAVDO meeting in Dakar. There are patronage operations also: they cite the example of Dr. Laryeah, a member of the GAPVOD Board, who is using some of the proceeds from his own medical clinic to run a rural village program.

2. PEA (People's Educational Association) was founded in 1949 and is affiliated with the University's Institute of Adult Education at Legon. It provides tutors for PEA branches, in continuing education, and programs that develop literacy and manual skills, social and community action. Funding is through the Institute of Adult Education at Legon and by Government, but, according to a 1985 report, no funding has been received in recent years. It has a national Executive Committee, but there has been no annual meeting for two years. Activities listed are "Literal" studies, GCE preparation, literacy courses, income generating projects such as soap making, fish farming, bee keeping, and the like.

3. AMASACHINA: This is a national, independent, voluntary organization formed in 1967 in rural areas. It does community awareness, self-help projects, mostly located in Western Dagomba   province of the North. It claims to have extremely good, cooperative relations with district govern-

ment officials, and the national Mobilization Committee, and the Ministries of Health, Education, Forestry, Department of Feeder Roads and local banks.

Their funds are self-generated but they get some from the Canadian High Commission and from the U.S. Embassy. In 1985-6 income was Cedis 545,000 (which then equalled $6,055). Much of its inputs come in kind, e.g., 8000 tree seedlings, machinery, equipment, food, communal labor from 10,000 people in 300 villages nation wide. The association provides administration, organization and mobilization of support after the village decides on a program -- for example, schools, health clinics, feeder roads, dams, reforestation, drainage programs. They built 13 primary schools in 1976-1984, adult education schools in two places, four health posts, 11 water dams (dugouts), and feeder roads in four places in 1985 alone. They also did reforestation with 8000 trees planted in 40 villages. In 1984, they made 12 bank loans, i.e., provided help to communities in getting these loans from a bank, and formed 18 women's coops, 14 of which got bank loans.

4. Christian Mothers Association. This organization was launched with $22,000 a year funding from The Konrad Adenauer Foundation with. It is associated with the self supporting Social Aid Guild of Ghana, which runs training schools. It is still funded by The Adenauer Foundation. This organization also has many individual groups of women, organized around work activities, e.g., market women's associations, etc. Some people claimed that this had been stimulated by Nkrumah's policies to get all the different groups organized, and that it was able to survive on its own.

5. Church Hospital Association of Ghana: is made up of churches that have hospitals, e.g., Catholic Church, Anglican, Methodist Church, the Church of Pentecost (itself an 1953 off-shoot of the Apostolic Church).

6. Ahmadiyya: This is an Islamic movement, that originated in what is now Pakistan and has influence in many parts of West Africa with 500,000 members in Ghana, and 4 million world wide.

7. Evangelical Presbyterian Church -- became independent in 1922 and has 300,000 members.

8. Grace Fellowship -- an off-shoot of the Ghana Baptist Church.

9. Christian Council of Ghana (also sometimes referred to as Council of Churches of Ghana?) -- which liaises with the World Council of Churches and plays a limited role as a funding agency or broker, for expenditure of Church World Services funds. Until 1980 it provided some of the same types

of services now provided by GAPVOD. Because, as such, it had no recognition by the Government, the tax exemptions etc. were obtained through the individual churches.   As the work got to be more complex, it was this organization that played a leading role in calling the conference that created the GAPVOD. One should note also that the current Executive Director of GAPVOD was formerly a staff member of the Council.

10. Committee on Church Participation in Development: Established in 1960, it was adopted by the Christian Council in 1963, and now serves as social welfare section of the Church Council.

11. Fellowship of Ghana Church Women: is interdenominational, funded by local contributions and by World Vision ($500 each quarter.)

There are a number of other indigenous VDO groups, such as the Boy Scouts, Girl Scouts, YMCA and YWCA which carry on activities typical of their counterparts elsewhere.

Expatriate Organizations:

Among the external VDOs, the Catholic Relief Service is exemplary of the contribution, problems and potential of these organizations. Following are comments from some of its leadership:

Catholic Relief Services (CRS):

The CRS has done its own directory of such agencies; it was completed last fall but has not yet been released. They feel that GAPVOD has been moribund but is now being reconstructed. Regarding coordination of VDOs, the Deputy Director of the organization felt he had learned most of what he knows elsewhere, outside the framework of his own office. He thinks there is relatively little coordination going on, not like in TOGO, where groups get allocated to specific regions.

CRS leadership believes there are an impressive number and variety of groups working in Ghana. An observer might be amazed at how many organizations are concentrated in the Tamale area as evidenced by the many different organization symbols one sees on the vehicles about town. One CRS leader said he could imagine people becoming a bit skeptical about the approach of external VDOs when seeing such a concentration of them. These organizations need to move beyond the rhetoric. The Headquarters of Caritas say they would work with other groups, but are skeptical about working under a ministry, where they likely would only get a request for a vehicle, i.e., the government people are not really serious! In 1987 the CRS supported about 110 Maternal and Child Health (MCH) centers, and provided food supplements, educational materials and growth monitoring services to 300 Primary Schools, Day Care Centers and Institutions for training the disabled.

As a result of decisions within CRS, the Ghana Program was being restructured. CRS would pull out of five regions and concentrate on the three Northern regions, which have the largest food deficits and greater need. After the restructuring, the emphasis will be on socio-economic projects that assist locally identified groups to upgrade their capabilities in various activities. CRS will look to the Ghana Education Service to take over the monitoring and supervisory activities of the institutional feeding programs for children, and to the Social Welfare Department under the Ministry of Mobilization and Productivity to supervise the food program for handicapped people. Once these ministries have identified counterpart personnel, the CRS will train them during an initial period of joint, side-by-side activity. After six months, when the counterpart personnel have had a chance to work by themselves, an evaluation will be conducted to determine if the monitoring activities can be turned over. These changes will reduce the workload of the CRS Nutrition Supervisors and permit them to concentrate on the MCH program, in order to upgrade its impact on the beneficiaries.

B. VDO Perceptions About Place -- Where the organizations are active:

The organizations active in Ghana are reasonably well spread around the country, in terms of their activities. The CRS directory lists 26 organizations that have programs in EACH of the ten regions of the country, only a few of which are associated with external governments or donor agencies, and most of which are indigenous, often Church-affiliated, organizations. The American and British volunteer programs operate throughout the country, whereas the French, Swiss, Korean, the EEC Fund are in only a few regions or operate only a generalized, national program. The Japanese volunteer service (the JOCV) is active in virtually all the regions.

Most organizations, however, have programs in only a few regions. A few, about 24, almost all of which are programs of external governments or agencies, and a few of which are official institutions of the Ghana Government, or are funded by it, operate general programs at the national level. The indigenous ones include the National Mobilization Committee and the National Center for Development Strategies, both of which are instruments of the Ghana Government. These were fairly recently created, as part of the "revolutionary government's" program of decentralization and grass roots empowerment.

The regions are generally equal in the number of active organizations, although the programs operated by external, development oriented volunteer organizations of the type that are our main concern in this study, tend to focus on the more needy regions of the country, mostly in the northern areas.

The major, external organizations are all well represented in these regions, for example, Oxfam, World Vision, Catholic Relief Services, Planned Parenthood, and a good many of the individual church organizations and foreign volunteer programs, such as the Peace Corps.

C. VDO Perceptions about Procedures

1. Registration:

The government requires VDOs to register as non-profit organizations, to state their aims and objectives, to be in the Registry General of Organizations (a ministry in itself). Those persons we interviewed knew of no organization that had been refused authorization. GAPVOD has questioned whether those on the register are all really development oriented and point out that several of the organizations on the registry list get direct subventions from the Ghana Government, such as the OIC, the YMCA and SOS Children.

In the Ministry of Finance and Economic Planning there is a small unit in the Manpower Division, with an officer assigned to work with the VDOs. In the near future, someone may even be seconded to the various VDOs. GAPVOD leaders have asked that this person should speak to one of their meetings, and think that a Deputy Minister has already given support to this request.

VDO leaders say that the government organs that have direct responsibility for relationships with them include the Ministry of Finance and Economic Planning (for general policy issues or technicalities, and issues of broad scope, e.g., discussions with the CRS about the reduction of their program here), the Division of International Economic Relations, the Manpower Division, the Ministry of Social Welfare, and the Registry of Social Organizations. In technical matters, the Ministries of Health, Education, Agriculture, etc. are also involved, as are the Ministry of Mobilization and Productivity (on labor issues, rights of the employees. etc.), the National Revenue Bureau, the Ghana Education Service, and for the food assistance programs, the Ministry of Education and the Ministry of Health, which groups like the CRS had to contact if they change aspects of their "Food and Nutrition Program").

2. Communication:

The Government departments that are supposed to know what VDOs are doing (and the discussion with GAPVOD leaders implied that they do know) are 1. The Registry 2. Social Welfare and Community Development and 3. Finance and Economic Planning.

CRS leadership says that the Ghana government doesn't require reports, but that they provide them nonetheless. CRS perceptions of GOG involvement with VDOs was illustrated by the issue of "recipient contributions" in the area of food and nutrition support. They believe that in the past the government was purchasing high protein foods for children at risk, but when CRS food supplementary programs came in, and given the budget constraints, the government virtually stopped supplying food. The National Nutrition Coordination Committee, a non-government body that advises government on nutrition policy at all stages of lunch programs and of which the CRS is a member, has decided that any organization supplying items for child feeding should get the approval of this committee first, to attest that the food conforms to a good nutritional standard of the WHO. GOG has also decided that all those doing nutrition and health education programs should use the same handbook.

CRS has held discussions with the Water and Sewage Corporation to talk about food for work and inputs into the water projects. Together they had worked it out at a rather advanced level, then CRS was restructured, and its own programs are being cut back, so the food and water projects are not likely to be carried forward.

3. Tax and import duty exemption:

The VDOs are supposed to be exempt from duties on items imported for their development work, and for the personnel involved, if the shipment arrives within six months of the arrival of the staff person involved. (See below for current perceptions of the problems with new procedures for imports by these organizations.)

4. The general freedom and appreciation of VDO contributions:

The GAPVOD Leadership feels that tradition and national character will protect the VDO sector (grass roots organizations) anyway. They assert that Ghana's policy orientation has been essentially the same since Nkrumah, one of pushing for self-help, self-reliance, power to the people, but this requires self-regulation and provision of information the government needs. In recent times the Government has been concerned about subversion. The way the VDOs should counteract such concerns is full disclosure of their activities and open discussion of their own needs and concerns, in the view of the GAPVOD leaders.

However, many VDO leaders feel that the government does not really recognize the VDO contribution to development. The VDOs need to connect better, to tell people what they are doing, to do the public relations work. The Niger approach of careful articulation of VDOs into local plans is reminiscent of Ghana in the 1950s when they had village or town development committees [48] but that approach failed completely because the program was really only rhetorical; there was no program planning, and no coordination, and virtually no real implementation. GAPVOD leadership felt that some sincere efforts were made; some success did occur, as indicated by the public's present willingness to continue to try that approach. They also had a rural electrification program, with installation of Indian generators in villages. That program also was not implemented -- only one or two plants ever got installed.

Although the government here is pushing for decentralization and devolution, one shouldn't expect a bureau to be created in the Head of State's office, such as the BSONG in Burkina-Faso.

D. Ghana VDO Perceptions Re: The Problems of Special Significance.

1. Tax exemption

VDOs are supposed to benefit from free entry of imports used in development work. But, the VDO leadership claims that recently the government has decided to tax ALL the organizations, across the board. We found this an exaggeration -- the government really has only decided to require a case-by-case justification on imports, because, shortly before our visit, an organization or two had been found importing things duty- free under this rubric and then selling them in the market. A family planning project, however, had cleared imports for its "May Day Project" with no difficulty. That organization's leadership told us, however, that now they have to apply anew for each shipment of imports.

VDO leadership opinion about the change in import duties seems to be in agreement that it is an important development. But some argued that the change may be related to a shipment (or a few items) of armaments that

---

[48] See the GAPVOD paper: *Collaboration for Participation*.

was discovered (i.e., a custom official may have found a gun in one shipment, but that could have been simply a hunting rifle).

They think that the GOG is also very sensitive about seeds that come in, and the dumping of drugs (from industrial countries). Recent flaps have worsened the situation for the Catholic Church, World Vision etc. But, exoneration from import duties etc. has not been a problem for a group like the CRS. They do have a person to follow the shipment, do routine clearance, to handle the bill of lading and deal with customs etc. TECH-NOSERVE was able to bring in a computer without difficulty.

GAPVOD has sent a memo to the PNDC, and the Ministries of Finance, Local Government Social Welfare etc. asking for restoration of tax/import exemptions. The memo referred to the Nairobi Statement (from the Enabling Environments Conference) as well as appealed to the "Decentralization" policy of the new government to justify this request, and refers to the decision of the Government. [49] The petition acknowledges that there had been abuses, but also points out that VDOs do complement government efforts at the grass roots levels in health, agriculture, family planning, etc., and estimates that they have brought "millions of dollars" into the country. The petition says that VDOs would be crippled by the new procedures, and their credibility reduced in their efforts to assist overseas agencies. With delays at the ports etc. there would be a hesitancy abroad to send materials. They asked the Government to consider GAPVOD as a vetting and clearing agency, as a coordinating body of these organizations, to vouch for the development character of the imports in question, and assure that these organizations do honor the government's policies.

GAPVOD claims that government people have visited them to arrange a meeting with the various groups concerned about the issue. They don't expect a "stepping back" for either aspect of the exemption. Moreover, only the indigenous VDOs seem to be affected at the moment. GAPVOD leaders believe that, given the previous laxity of policy/practices, virtually anyone could set up a so-called Voluntary Development Program and could bring things in duty free. Therefore, it is a good idea to move to regularize these procedures and to have the government know what is really going on.

---

[49] However, when we asked various Government officials to give us a decree or law number or reference, no-one knew of any. The decision may simply have been announced, or the various officials may simply not know what the proper reference is.

CARITAS is also trying, without success, to get something in writing about the government's formula for calculating income tax obligations (e.g., for their staff). They have paid it, and are not objecting to it, but want to know how the calculation is made. The matter came up when CARITAS raised a question about the amount of the tax, and found an error, which government admitted. But the government hasn't responded to their inquiry about just how the calculation was made in the first place. CARITAS leaders said they had been waiting six weeks with no response.

2. Lack of Government Attention:

The government has supervisory staff to monitor health and service programs such as those supported by the CRS, but often times they are not mobile. In the case of the CRS, the monthly travel plans of its personnel are copied to the Regional Directorate and to supervisory staff of the Ministry of Health. Whenever possible, plans are made for CRS and MOH supervisory staff to travel together on inspections. However, for various reasons (perhaps including insufficient government per-diem payments to the government personnel) MOH supervisory staff are not always able to stay overnight on these treks, and thus they are not able to travel with the CRS staff as often as they may wish.

The CRS claims to inform regional government bureaus of each visit to the site of its projects, especially where government staff or institutions are involved, in order to inform these bureaus of the CRS activities. It seems, however, that NGOs/VDOs seldom get any reaction from government personnel to their reports.

The net result of this situation is that, often, the government has to rely on an NGO or VDO inspection or evaluation of activities of considerable importance, such as feeding facilities, where public health issues are involved.

D. VDO Perceptions about Prospects

GAPVOD perceptions of special opportunities for VDOs include:

--Trends toward an external interest in funding local Foundations, on-granting facility. As a potential recipient of external block-grants or funds for on-granting, Ghanaian VDO leaders cite their own Rural Development Fund which could become a multi-purpose fund, because almost all the projects are rural.

-- With the Government's new Public Investment Program (PIF) and perhaps with the Rural Development Fund also in mind, the Government asked GAPVOD to submit a proposal for strategic planning, including policy and planning for government support (assuming the recipients abide by the code of conduct and requirements of government recognition). This would include their (and other VDOs') participation in the general planning process. Existing VDO projects do complement government priorities, but until now there is no really formal and detailed process of fitting these projects into the Plan, especially at local levels.

        -- The International organizations: the GAPVOD is aware that the UNDP is interested in doing a directory, but did not comment on funding possibilities with them, or on relationships with other international donors. They seemed unaware that the fourth UNDP Country Program would provide many opportunities for promoting VDO activity. Nor were they aware of an impending, major USAID/UNDP mission to assess ways to promote VDO work.

III. Perceptions by Ghana Government and International Agency Officials

A. Government Perceptions about The Actors -- People/Product:

     1. Indigenous Organizations:

Ghana government officials in the Ministry of Finance and Economic Planning (MFEP) had been contacted by various VDOs, including the federation, GAPVOD, but a number of officials there were relatively ill-informed about the characteristics and activities of this sector. An official with USAID faults the VDOs themselves, saying that they don't do the necessary public relations work. He thought that they are doing more than the government realizes and would be more appreciated if what they do were better known.

     2. Expatriate Organizations:

The Government has a very limited view of the VDO sector. The only recent contact of one of the bureaus charged with monitoring relations with the VDOs, was in October 1986 with one of the expatriate organizations, the British Overseas Volunteers Service (OVS, a British Government program like the Peace Corps). That organization's representative was just now seeking to regularize their authorization despite the fact that they had already been operating in the country since the 1950s. The meeting was at OVS initiative and had to do with restoring exoneration of imports and taxes etc. following the changes in governmental practice. The particular ministry official was not sure, however, just how long the OVS had operated in the country, nor was he able to recount the discussion without going through the files.

Other volunteer programs the office knew about were the U.S. Peace Corps, the Japanese volunteer program, which is considered one of the most active in Ghana since 1978 or 1979, and the U.N. volunteer program, to which Ghana mostly sends out volunteers, rather than receiving them. That aspect is changing now as the UN program comes to involve a more sophisticated type of volunteer. The CRS program was described as providing only one government health worker at the local level, but little at national or regional levels. The German program was thought to be "fizzling out".

The most visible nutrition programs are being sponsored by UNICEF, USAID, the Japanese aid program, and VDOs such as CRS, ADRA, World Vision International, Oxfam-UK, and Meals for Millions.

3. Government Agencies:

According to informed observers among the international agencies, the VDO community, and some government bureaus, the Ghana Government does not have many dealings with VDOs, as already noted. The Government is only minimally involved, if at all, in the implementation of VDO projects. It admits that it has not really accorded this whole area the seriousness it deserves.

It is plainly evident to the casual observer in Ghana today that government bureaus are not highly productive. Although many individuals are conscientious and busy, many plainly are not. One problem in this regard is that salaries are now extremely low and many people feel there is no incentive for higher productivity.

The VDOs have not collaborated much among themselves as well. The push to expand this sector and enhance its organization is coming from external agencies, like the UNDP, not from the Ghana Government, at least so far. The government has no mechanism to include VDOs in projects submitted to or already funded by the UNDP, although the latter, like other external agencies, now tends to favor VDOs because of prospects of quicker and more efficient action. The UNDP is pushing the VDOs to relate better to the donors, who meet once a month.
At the time of the interviews for this study, the UNDP was expecting an important study mission to assess prospects for greater support and use of the VDO sector. The mission, financed by UNDP and PACT, was expected to spend a week in Ghana and visit several other countries as well. It would focus on conditions favorable to and unfavorable to cooperation among and

with PVOs, Government, and the UNDP. It was to explore the existing and potential areas of activity, and assess the coordination structures and needs. There is the possibility of a Round Table that includes the VDO sector, and other innovative institutional arrangements. This mission study should complement an assessment of the social impact of Ghana's structural adjustment program, that was recently finished as a result of the UNICEF challenge to the World Bank over the social impact of structural adjustment programs. That effort has produced a Plan of Social Action (PAMSCAA) which will provide an enlarged role for VDOs.

A Government Memo [50] dealing with the coming UNDP mission says that the mission will cover a) conditions favorable or constraining to UN-DP/NGO/govt collaboration for grass roots development, b) nature, extent of NGO activity or local capability especially to work with NGOs, and, c) congruence between UNDP and government program priorities and NGO priorities/capability, d) UNDP field office experiênce with NGOs, e) existing collaboration efforts among UNDP/NGO/government and institutional arrangements, f) potential areas for substantive cooperation within countries and at regional levels, g) work with selected NGOs to determine ways in which they could help implement a government program of action and measures to address the social cost of adjustment (PAMSCAA).

B. Government Perceptions of Spacial Location:

There was little commentary on this aspect of the VDO situation in Ghana, other than to be noted as a concern by one of the ranking officials in the Ministry of Finance and Economic Planning.

C. Government Perceptions of Procedures:

1. Registration/Authorization

A new VDO might be violating a technical regulation but would not really suffer significant consequences to go directly to a locality, set up shop and work with local groups that might invite them to do so. If the VDO is carrying out a special project, it might have to have direct relations with the relevant technical ministry, and they might have direct discussions with Finance, but still not have to go through any local machinery. Those that set up through Churches might rely on the tax exemption and other official relations to cover their operations.

---

[50] Ghana Government Document UND/4/00 #14 of 27 July 1987.

So far, there is no single, overall governmental coordinating mechanism for the VDOs. Overall responsibility is with the Ministry of Finance and Economic Planning (MFEP), but it is being restructured. The various relevant technical ministries would also want to be involved in plans for VDO activity in their domain. The VDOs are supposed to report to this ministry but do not, and little is done about that. The International Economic Relations Department of the MFEP is beginning to compile its own directory of all the NGOs and their interests. Its United Nations desk has supervisory responsibility for most of the external VDOs because their relief activities fall mostly under the UN system.

2. Communication:

The GOG is clearly still in the formative stages of regularizing its relations with the VDO sector, and so communications with it are sporadic and haphazard. The GAPVOD may be able to ameliorate this situation if it can become more active and organized, with publications and meetings. So far, there has been only the occasional meeting between the GAPVOD leadership and government officials, the GAPVOD forum of many years ago, and a very rudimentary newsletter.

The GOG officials with responsibility for relations with VDO type organizations feel there is a problem with respect to their adequate monitoring of VDOs. The planning agencies don't know who or what the VDOs are, or what they are doing. Government officials claimed that they do not want to interfere with these organizations, or deprive them of their independence, but that there is a concern about their concentration in some areas. They feel it would be difficult to track all the organizations down. One official thought there had been a meeting in October 1986 devoted to how the organizations should liaise with the government. GAPVOD has claimed it organized such a meeting, but there was little evidence of any impact from it among those we interviewed.

3. Taxes/Import Duty Payments

It is the responsibility of each VDO to negotiate its own country agreement, which until very recently provided a blanket exoneration from taxes and import duties for personal effects and imports relating to the program of the organizations. The agreements are now being done on an organization by organization basis because the Government thinks there have been abuses, and, evidently, the Government's revenue needs are greater. It seems that few or no exemptions are being given at the moment. Government claims they had instances of organizations using their exemption to bring in goods which they then commercialized. So now it will be difficult to get the exemption agreements, even for the Church organizations. Exemptions for the official volunteers must be applied for by each organization.

Where items supplied by USAID to the VDOs for development activities are concerned, however, the Ghana government still does have to clear them through customs on the basis of the existing "blanket agreement" which covers all USAID imports. For example, items it consigns to the CRS are all duty free. USAID does not get into the picture, nor does it make any recommendations regarding other groups or activities it is not directly financing. USAID will not front for these organizations, even if they are American. The USAID office recalled no instance of obtaining a tax or import exoneration for an organization, per se, through use of the USAID blanket agreement with the Ghana Government.

4. Freedom for VDOs:

Government officials point to the decentralization, or "devolution" program now going on as favoring VDOs and grass roots action. This program is in the political domain. One official remarked that if people have political power, they can determine their own economic program at the grass roots level. Resources do exist at the local level, but actors there need a sense of direction and need to be creative. Local people have done well there already, if one can get them organized, not in the sense of thinking for them. These people know their own priorities and what they want and need, he said. Assistants should provide them with what would help them to develop themselves. "The local people, peasants, are the guys that have carried the country on their backs, and they are getting less and less. There is abject poverty at local levels."

He further asserted that the elite has been able to allocate a disproportionate share of the national resources to itself because they are articulate, visible, and well organized. Small village protests are not noticed. Emphasis on village-level action is needed. The country needs now to address the social cost of adjustment programs. The driving force here is really the vulnerable groups problem of structural adjustment, the need to regularize this sector and have the VDOs as allies, such as VSO and bilateral volunteer agencies like the Peace Corps.

We note that these views seem to reflect impact from the UNICEF campaign, which has one of its more active officers/ offices in Accra.

5. Funding:

The UNDP expects to have substantial funding for VDO activities and is seeking to help get this sector organized, whereupon the scope and nature of such funding would become clearer.

Some indigenous and the U.S. VDOs can get some funding from the USAID, in the form of matching grants and contracts to handle the distribution of relief supplies. The matching grants are worked out as one overall global Foreign Volunteer Assistance program, and so can't be counted on in any given locality. There is acknowledgement of food assistance coming in, (USAID says about 40m Cedies worth) and the USAID wants to allow VDO use of the counterpart funds generated by its distribution. Food aid acts as a balance-of-payments support for Ghana's structural adjustment program, and helps to overcome some of the real hardships the program has caused. It is used for relief and for development purposes. However, American Food Aid results as much from pressures in America to dispose of its grain surpluses as from need in Ghana.

The USAID thinks that VDOs can get small grants from something like CODEL, an umbrella grant arrangement, and from USAID matching grants, such as have already gone to some U.S. organizations, including but not necessarily limited to TECHNOSERVE, Salvation Army, World Vision, and CRS, which has some Title II money. In the past, OIC has had some funding, as did Apple, for community and rural development work. GOVA got a small grant from PACT, which itself receives a good deal of U.S. Government funding.

AID argues against using hard currency to meet local currency costs, as happens with a lot of the VDO activity. If they used local funds they could bring in more imports needed elsewhere in the society. However, in the past the GOG has not been very interested in that.

6. Fit with Plan:

There was a meeting of donors in September 1987, in preparation for a later, formal conference of donors, possibly in Norway in early 1988, concerning a program of "Priority Action to Mitigate the Social Cost of Adjustment." Such a program might help harmonize the inputs of VDOs also. The official review of the most recent planned investment program was that not enough notice had been taken of the smaller scale, e.g., VDO, projects that have social impact aspects of relevance. This is why the MFEP is trying to correct this situation and to promote a more organized VDO action for inclusion in the next report. Government is also reviewing the general investment code.

The Water and Sewerage Department has been especially vocal on the need for VDOs to cooperate and consult with them before they carry out field projects. Problems have already been confronted with regard to VDO water projects not meshing into the governments efforts. The problems included: 1) distribution of the systems; 2) some groups digging wells only in certain locations because of their good political connections, even with external government agencies, whereas other regions might have greater need for wells. There has also been a problem of the use of different types of equipment from what the government or other sponsors were using, preventing appropriate linkages between local projects.

D. Government Perception of Problems:

1. Tax/duties:

We have already noted the changes being implemented regarding tax and duty exemptions for VDOs, as perceived by the VDO leadership. Government officials generally confirmed their perception of a tightening of the procedures, but, disconfirmed the notion that all imports would now be taxed. The essence of the change is that each group must justify the development relevance of each import. So far, however, no group has been refused import-tax exemption for development program equipment or inputs.

2. Government Tolerance of and Attention to VDOs:

The government officials we interviewed are acutely aware that the structural adjustment program has really taxed the society and caused considerable hardship. They believe that the VDOs may be very useful in countering these effects, and so want to promote their role, but on a more knowing and regularized basis. The government claims to be trying to raise the recognition of VDOs that there is a governmental agency that has overall responsibility for this sector. On the other hand, external donor agencies, such as the UNDP and the USAID, claim to have had to push the Government to encourage greater roles for the VDOs, and to allow them into local areas. USAID has especially tried to feel out the government about providing for the use of some of the accumulated counterpart funds for VDO programs.

E. Government Perceptions of Prospects for VDO Activity:

1. General Funding:

The International Economic Relations Division of the MFEP is engaged in examining a range of projects and potentialities for addressing the key social sector concerns arising from the structural adjustment program, as we have mentioned. In this connection its preparations for the September 1987 visit of the UNDP mission on VDOs reveals something of the government's orientation toward providing or facilitating more funding for the VDOs. The suggestion is for a rural social action investment program based on a dossier of social and developmental impact projects at the rural level and sponsored by local communities. It would be separated from the PIP by its funding character. No VDO is specifically included in the present one, either as plan or report. The Government will try to address that next year; it is a rolling plan. A percentage of the funding will come from the initiators at the local level and the rest from the govt matching funds, donor aid and VDOs. The aim is to capture initiatives and find resources not normally available to government. The administration of the project will be non-governmental but the supervision will and must be by the government, possibly at the District level of administration. [51]

A GOG memorandum on this subject argues that a rural action investment program - The PIP - is moving into the phase of taking on more socially-impacting projects with funding from donors and GOG. The effort emphasizes national projects, primarily, and is based on the belief that the Government should move toward having a national dossier of projects and programs geared to impact on urban and rural poor, concentrating on rural areas, so as to draw urban poor to the rural areas. Donors are thought to accept rural and social sector impacting programs, but to emphasize economically impacting projects. NGOs however, operate programs basically with social and development impact, as opposed to economic ones. The GOG admits its lack of well articulated dossiers of such projects and the absence of a conscious strategy to harness resources for rural and social sector impacting programs. [52]

The UNDP has begun a listing of viable projects for co-financing by donors. This may not get very far because most donors prefer to have their own projects. The answer appears to be to have a national dossier of projects and programs geared to impacting on urban and rural poor. There are some on-going rural action programs, such as the EEC's "micro project scheme" for schools, day care centers etc., but they contain no explicit mention of the role of VDOs.

---

[51] Ghana Government Document, UND/4/100 #13. of 27 July 1987.

[52] *Ibid.*

2. On-Granting Facilities: The USAID says they have on the drawing board a preliminary organization of national resource management programs in response to concerns for environmental problems and hazards (desertification, erosion, tree felling, etc.) and are proposing a modest project in which American and indigenous PVOs would submit projects in those specific areas. This would be something like a PVO umbrella project, but here, focussed on natural resource management. Other examples of umbrella grants are to be found in Kenya, Chad, the Sahel region, Zaire and the Philippines, and Sri Lanka.

3. New Areas of Opportunity: With respect to bi-lateral program possibilities the Ghana Government signals that the USAID PL480 and such programs could lead to a "social sector grant facility". The idea is to incorporate the small projects, including those of VDOs into the Public Investment Programme (PIP), which is a three-year program. The existing 1986-1988 plan has been criticized on social projects grounds because these are not considered investment, or because they are so small.

The Ghana Government noted [53] that the USAID had offered to give support with PL480 counterpart funds to projects and programs that alleviate the impact of retrenchment, such as on people losing jobs because of a cutback in the size of government and para-statal employment. Government officials think that this is because the donors want to avoid bearing the onus of the retrenchment programs they have been advocating. With respect to multilateral program possibilities, the UNDP is considering promoting NGO (VDO) activity in its future funding cycle.

---

[53] See document UND/4/100 #13 of 27 July 1987.

CHAPTER IV.

VDOs/NGOs AND WOMEN IN DEVELOPMENT

I. Statements Indicating Heightened Consciousness

There is evidence of VDO's heightened consciousness regarding the participation of women in development, but there are relatively few VDO projects involving women and there are relatively few women employed as "development professionals". This disparity in women's participation in projects and employment holds true for Northern/International NGOs and Southern VDO's. Heightened consciousness regarding the so called Women's Issue in development most frequently takes the form of statements such as: l) a statement regarding women's contribution to the area under discussion, like the fact that the majority of food producers in Africa are women; 2) a statement indicating women's relative exclusion within the topic being discussed, such as the fact that there are few VDO projects involving women, or; 3) statements of concern from a "caucus" of women at a meeting pointing out their low-level of representation in the meeting.

Northern NGOs note that they frequently encounter male resistance in Third World field projects designed to raise the socio-economic status of women. However, Southern VDOs, while not denying the myriad problems women encounter in Third World countries, note that if they are to trust Northern NGO's statements regarding their belief in the importance of involving women in development in the Third World, they must first see enormous improvement in the North in the number of women involved in their own organizations at high levels. The problem continues to be a significant one as shown by the Statement on behalf of women participants at an International NGO conference held in November 1985 in Geneva:

"...speaking on behalf of a group of women at this conference - I stress not all women ....to express the frustration and disappointment which we have felt with this meeting. ...we draw your attention to the fact that, among the chair people, the rapporteur and the panels, there has been minimal involvement of women....also applies to the resource inputs...wonder why the working documents...have all been prepared by men from Northern NGOs." [54]

At a meeting of the Development Assistance Committee planning a Seminar on the role of NGOs in agriculture and rural development in Africa, held near the same time in Paris, a female delegate noted that questions concerning women's groups were totally absent in the preparatory documentation available. She asserted that Governments had often failed to notice the share of production due to the female labor force in Africa and expressed the hope that such an omission would not be repeated at the Seminar. [55]

These statements demonstrate that despite heightened consciousness illustrated by statements indicating women's contribution or noting their omission, women are still frequently excluded from VDO activity in terms of participation in international meetings and in participation in field project activity.

II. Statements Acknowledging the Significant Economic Role of African Women

A. Enabling Environment Conference Statement

There is both increased acknowledgement of the significant economic role of African women and there are great expectations regarding the ability of VDOs to increase active participation of women in their development projects as seen in statements such as the following which comes from the report of the Enabling Environment Conference on Effective Private Sector Contribution to Development in Sub-Saharan Africa. The Conference urges Private Development Agencies to:

"Recognize the critical role that women play in Africa's development and assist them with access to credit, special extension services, appropriate technology and relief from discriminatory practices. "[56]

---

[54] Final Report, "NGOs and Africa: A Strategy Workshop," NGLS/-Geneva. November, 1985, p. 66.

[55] DAC Meeting, November, 1985 presentation by Canadian representative.

[56] An NGO FORUM organizer's statement.

Similarly, The African NGO Forum indicates an expectation for enhancing the quality of life for women in their development activities by including the following recommendation in its strategy statement for overcoming the African crises:

> "*Sixth*, when it comes to food production, due regard must be paid to the fact that the bulk of the food producers in Africa are women. Therefore, their legal rights to land, as well as their right to participate fully in all decision-making and allocation of resources must be respected and recognized."[57]

C. International Agencies' Statements

A newsletter of the World Hunger Education Service (June-July 1986) provided an interesting synthesis of the major findings of seven agencies concerned with addressing the African crises.[58] Three issues emerged from the seven reports: 1) food security; 2) internal distributional problems with the costs and benefits of development strategies in general and of adjustment policies in particular; and 3) the role of export crops in relation to both of these concerns. The summarization of the reports with regard to women is instructive:

> "Women are mentioned as a specific population category only in regard to population policies by the World Bank's report. Each of the other reports, reflecting again their greater attention to social analysis and greater distributional precision, refer to the important economic role of African women. Women are viewed as the 'majority of the food producers' (Committee on African Development Strategies), who dominate food production in most countries (OAU), producing from 50 to 80 percent of food and other crops (InterAction). Women also play a key role in African economies as 'managers of household resources' (UNICEF). One of the few significant economic changes to take place in Zimbabwe since

---

[57] African NGO Preparatory Meeting, Nairobi, 12-15 April, 1986. "Position Paper of African Non-Governmental Organizations on The Critical Economic Situation in Africa," presented to the Special Session of the U.N. General Assembly, May 16, 1986. p. 6.

[58] The seven agencies are: The World Bank, The Organization of African Unity, UNICEF, the Committee on African Development Strategies, InterAction, Worldwatch Institute, and Church Drought Action in Action.

independence, according to the Churches Drought Action in Africa, is 'some predominantly female cooperatives production of local consumer goods'. Worldwatch insists that, for reforestation programs to succeed, women must be included as foresters and community organizers." [59]

III. Heightened Expectations for Indigenous VDO Action

Given the significance of the acknowledged importance of the economic role of African women, it would seem that programs involving women would be very high priority in economic development plans. However, such is not the case. But, the statements by international agencies calling for greater attention to women's involvement offer challenges to all VDO planners, strategists, programmers, to go beyond statements to action.

What is frequently lacking is evidence of well-developed programs which integrate women into planning, implementation, and evaluation of all activities rather than occasional women's programs. Indeed, special programs for women are called for. Such is always the need for any group which has historically been excluded. But the point heard frequently from proponents wishing to enhance the quality of women's lives, is that such special programs cannot serve as the excuse for not including women in the mainstream of programming. It is this challenge that has not been fully accepted by NGOs, North or South. The challenge is extraordinarily difficult to accept because it represents a fundamental change in a wide range of social customs and beliefs governing male-female relationships. But the significant economic and social roles of women have been frequently acknowledged and the present economic crises in Africa is very severe. Therefore, much greater attention must be paid to improving the quality of life for women in all their roles if development is to become reality.

The agencies most admired for their innovative, participatory, cost-effective methods in development activities are NGOs and indigenous African VDOs have stated that development is their responsibility. They must, therefore, create more effective programs which integrate women into planning, implementation, and evaluation of all activities.

IV. Promising Models of Support for Women in Development

A. AFOTEC

---

[59] *Hunger Note*, Newsletter of the World Hunger Education Service, June-July, 1986. p. 3.

There are some VDOs, international as well as indigenous, which have some approaches, programs and projects offering positive models of support for women in development. One such model is an indigenous African VDO which has women highly placed in its structure and stresses programs for women.   It's not a women's project, but responds to the challenge of the inclusion of women in its mainstream programming. The VDO's philosophy can be heard in the following statement by its female Director:

"One is always hearing talk of the 'integration of women into development activities'.   But that is not really the point. Women are already the leading participants in all development activities in Africa, given their key role in the major aspects of economic, social and cultural life.   They are in fact producers, traders, wives, mothers, teachers, all at the same time. They are at the forefront of the agricultural production which is at the heart of the economy in all the African countries. The real problem lies in the recognition at its true worth of the primordial role played by women and the identification of the specific and appropriate means which need to be applied so that they can improve the conditions and the environment in which they carry out their tasks, for their own benefit and that of their communities." [60]

This VDO director's organization clearly emphasizes women's groups. However, she also stresses that their programming applies to both men and women because she says:

"If stress is sometimes placed on the specific problems of women, this is always put in the context of the community as a whole, since the practice of applying solutions in isolation to the problems of women has done much to marginalize the large minority they represent and the actions undertaken in their favor." [61]

Instead of treating women in isolation, therefore, this VDO takes as a starting point questions from groups within a community. But, the Director goes on to say:

"...it is not only questions we receive. There are also thoughts and proposals. And increasingly, by sheer force of circumstance, the

---

[60] R. Tall. "AFOTEC - An African N.G.O..." O.E.C.D. Development Cooperation Directorate document # DCD/86/25. p. 18.

[61] *Ibid*. p. 3.

men are increasingly backing up these questions. Some are saying 'the women have courage but everything depends on them', while a frequently heard leitmotif in the group meetings is 'our wives are tired...'. Given the fact that the women play such a prominent role,...any serious attempt to help the groups acquire the where-withal for their independence inevitably requires that priority be given to increased support for women, who seem at present to be the only channel for possible change....In Africa, the women play a major role in the production, preserving, processing and marketing of agricultural products, especially food crops....And yet, they have no access to improved technology, to agricultural training, to credit, all of which are usually channelled to cash crops and the making of profits. For some years now the questions coming from women and from the groups on these subjects have become increasingly nume-rous: ...where to find the loan needed to buy the plough for the rice-field, how to get the money to launch the small trading activity to offset to some extent the bad harvests, how to find the time and the energy to get through all the daily tasks (the working day already lasts 15 or 16 hours), and so on." [62]

The response of this indigenous VDO is a combination of training, project assistance and applied research. Training for women has included: weighing of foodstuffs, construction of improved stoves, production of hand-operated water-pumps. (All 55 of the women who have been trained have made a pump and installed it in their own village.) [63]

B. Le Comité International des Femmes Africaines Pour le Développement (CIFAD)

Another positive model of support for women in development is an indigenous African VDO which is a coordination committee for associations of women's groups in French-speaking Africa, CIFAD. The Coordinating committee was formed at Forum 85 in Nairobi as a result of the feeling of solidarity and need for organized action expressed by African women during that meeting. Therefore, the first activity of CIFAD was a workshop at Forum 85 presenting the problems of development confronted by African women. Of concern was the fact that decisions about needs and projects are made almost unilaterally by donor agencies. Also of concern was the need

---

[62] R. Tall. "AFOTEC..." op.cit., p. 9.

[63] *Ibid*. p. 12.

for networking and exchange between women's groups on the continent and with women's groups elsewhere.

Women from francophone African countries created a Permanent Committee for Coordination with the associations of women in the following countries: Benin, Burkina Faso, Cameroon, Congo, The Central African Republic, Côte d'Ivoire, Gabon, Guinea-Conakry, Mali, Morocco, Mauritania, Niger, Rwanda, Senegal, Togo, Tunisia, and Zaire.   The goal of the organization is to support and promote women's active participation and effective integration into all aspects of African socio-economic development. The specific objectives of the organization are the following:

- -identify and promote women's development projects which improve the conditions of their lives,
- -promote exchange of information regarding the development of such projects,
- -encourage training and research related to development projects,
- -establish an international network of support for development projects,
- -identify and solicit funding for women's development projects from supportive organizations.

CIFAD has received support from several Canadian NGOs and the Government of Côte d'Ivoire. Such Government connection is not frequently seen in Africa. In this case, the Ministry of Women's affairs in Côte d'Ivoire has provided staff time and other resources in support of an VDO still in the developmental stage. Since CIFAD has presently no permanent staff other than a secretary, and is currently trying to raise funds for a full staff, Government support is very important to keep the organization moving and enable it to carry on some program activities. This type of Government Ministry support provides a positive example of "development" which is not always stressed because it is not considered grassroots development. But clearly, if indigenous African VDOs are to be in a better position to assist grassroots development, the VDOs must themselves receive the support necessary to sustain their activities. The African government assistance given to CIFAD is then an example of the "partnership" relationship requested by indigenous African VDOs at their Forum meeting in Dakar in May 1987.

Staff on loan from the Ministry has been able to make initial visits to most of the member countries to reinforce contacts, learn about women's activities and highlight the existence of CIFAD and its potential as a support mechanism for their development programs. A Permanent Coordination Committee office of CIFAD has been set up in Abidjan, and two activities have been undertaken, a General Assembly meeting and a seminar entitled "Média, Femmes et Développement".

The President of CIFAD noted that there is a representative of the organization in each member country, but not a branch of CIFAD requiring a formal protocol within the country.   She also said she has been well received by government officials in all the member countries she has visited because CIFAD is designed to provide support and funding of projects selected by women's organizations, not to select projects itself, so, she said, "People naturally welcome support of their efforts."

CHAPTER V.

CONCLUSIONS

The general evolution of discussion among African VDO groups and leaders, and their interaction with similar groups in the Northern countries demonstrates the maturation of organized volunteerism and private sector leadership in Africa. These organizations and leaders find themselves delicately balanced between an aggressive and resourceful, and potentially stifling although well-meaning external community of allies, and their own governments which are not only still relatively ill-informed about their activities, but perhaps fearful of their potential social, and thus political, power.

Our examination of the perspectives of leaders in both circles, the VDOs and Officialdom, a reveal some potentially serious problems of communication and perspective, as well as considerable mutual appreciation. We summarize the implications as follows:

I. The Actors

VDOs are commonly perceived to be and are valued by citizenry, governments and themselves as non-profit, formal organizations, whose development activities involve a high degree of voluntary participation in activities intended to improve the economic and social wellbeing and/or productivity of the ordinary citizenry, usually in the rural areas.

There tends to be a distinct difference of definition and perception between the international, and especially the Western Industrial Country official agencies and NGOs and the Africans about whether VDOs necessarily are non-governmental. The nomenclature is a bit unsettled in Africa. NGO or PVO is an established part of the parlance of the United Nations and Western governments, but African governments, especially, question the relevance of these terms to the array of village level associations and cooperatives, or informal improvement associations in Africa, and question the "non-governmental" character of the many Northern organizations that receive the bulk of their material resources from their home governments.

It is evident to everyone that there has been a proliferation of NGOs/-VDOs active in Africa in recent years. They number in the many hundreds, and have brought very significant financial resources into Africa at times of great need. U.S.-based PVO organizations brought nearly one half billion dollars into Africa during 1984 alone. However, there is great fear, not unreasonable, that the NGO/PVO/VDO factor will turn out to be a "flash-in-the-pan" phenomenon. During the height of the drought, with dramatic media coverage of great misery, there was an outpouring of public philanthropy. As Africa recovers, and as the public has come to be habituated, or even bored with the issue, funding has fallen off. Although many are well established, most are of recent creation. Most are external, and almost all the indigenous ones depend on external financing. Development programs that assume high levels of PVO funding and VDO activity may fall apart. Africa confronts a new pending dependency and vulnerability. In response, Government and societal leaders alike are calling for the use of local organizations to carry out development projects, for the hiring by the external organizations of local people at all levels, including the general management of the local projects, and representation in the central staffs. They also believe that their own university graduates should be used to do the types of jobs that so often are given to expatriate personnel with no greater training.

II. Terms of Reference

Between the VDOs and the host institutions, there is no stable, common set of terms of reference for VDO activity. Especially the Western VDOs imagine themselves to be among the most effective and efficient providers of development services and finance, and to be agents for broad-scale social change and mobilizers of local initiative and resources. They have a self-image of being carriers of new, modern, values and skills. They tend to believe that governmental and especially larger scale development programs have almost all failed and that Governments generally are not concerned to advance the common people and vulnerable groups, e.g., marginal ethnic and subordinate social groups, such as women. They often feel these convictions are shared by the local people with whom they work. On the other hand, however much the VDOs may criticize the governmental agencies for neglecting women, for example, the VDOs themselves continue to have poor records in actually putting women in charge of the organizations, or of projects in the field.

The VDOs want to be left alone to do their job, with less bureaucratic formalism and fewer delays in approvals. They want to have direct contact with local areas and be able to concentrate on small-scale projects elaborated by them in direct contact with local people. They tend to think that projects that come to them from governmental agencies do not result from popular demands or represent the interests of politically impotent groups or areas. They think that the Government's motivation for requiring frequent reporting and contact with local officials is to achieve complete surveillance and domination of the VDOs and the local people. The VDOs want to be treated as serious development resources, and thus exonerated from various import, value-added and other taxes, as are most official aid programs and projects.

The host African official institutions tend to appreciate the resources and good-will of the VDOs, and in the many cases where these organizations have evolved from earlier religious, confessional and missionary institutions, have welcomed the evolution of their activity into secular enterprise and social service. The governments generally express satisfaction with the growth of VDO resources, especially from abroad, and tend to consider them as supplementary to traditional official development assistance flows.

But, African officials have also expressed some negative reactions to the VDO phenomenon. They are wary of a frequent lack of cultural understanding and adaptation on the part of external VDO personnel, and their sometimes brusk manners and impatience, and insistence on organizational and operational independence. African government officials have shown some intolerance of the emergence of internal VDOs of any substantial scope. They are disquieted by the scattered location, seemingly piece-meal character and insignificant economic impact of much of the VDO development activity when considered individually.

The African governments are calling for longer term financial commitments. They want greater harmonization and concertation of activities among the VDOs and with the official development plan institutions and perspectives. They question the professional qualifications of many of the VDO personnel (external and indigenous) and increasingly accuse external VDOs of "transferring to Africa unemployment from abroad," with regard to their own staff, and wish greater use to be made of local unemployed university graduates. The governments insist on registration of these organizations and approval of each project, and tend to want fuller disclosure and more regular reporting on past operational activities and their future project plans.

III. Communications Problems

Communication problems between the VDOs and host Governments are numerous but diminishing. The VDOs have increasingly joined together in federations or information-clearing- house type associations at the national level, to facilitate communication with each other and negotiation with official institutions. USAFA, Live Aid/Band Aid and the UNDP have stimulated such cooperation. Governments are also moving toward simpler, singular contact or supervisory offices to facilitate coordination and communication. African VDOs seem constantly to feel the need to stress their loyalty to and partnership with governmental development aims and programs. The African VDOs are also coming to create international structures for communication and collaboration among themselves and more effective partnership and interaction with external organizations that tend to have many more means and opportunities than they have for common planning and interaction.

IV. Shift in Funding Patterns?

Western donors are expanding their funding for activity by their own national VDOs working abroad, and are exploring ways for direct funding of indigenous VDOs. On the other hand, prior to reversals caused by popular sensitivities to the impact of drought and famine in 1984 and 1985, levels of official aid, bi-laterally and through multi-lateral institutions, had been declining. A shift to funding to and through VDOs may not arrest, but could disguise the longer term downward trend line of external development assistance to Africa.

New institutional arrangements for funding to VDOs may also be emerging. The Canadian and Scandinavian governments have supported local mechanisms (that involve indigenous organizations in decision making) for on-granting to local recipients. Some African and Western governments and U.N. agencies are exploring para-statal like arrangements for financing VDO work, that would link local and external official, multi-lateral and VDO sources. For some time the USAID has had guidelines for funding of local VDOs.

V. The Missing Concerns

Surprisingly, both Government and VDO leaders failed to raise a number of issues that have concerned, and often troubled, analysts and leaders of political processes, including the promotion of political and economic development, when considered in a broader context. Some of these issues are of special concern to development-planners with respect to the larger scale operations that have been undertaken by Governments and institutions like the World Bank or the African Development Bank. In the future, similar concerns may prove to be of significance for the VDO operations as well. We think it especially important to note the following such issues:

A. Catalysts for Broad-scale Change

There seemed to be little concern about the supposedly enormous potential contribution of NGOs/PVOs/VDOs to the mobilization, organization and representation of ordinary people for greater influence on and control over the institutions and activities that significantly impact their lives, whether they emanate from the Government, the party, or other authorities. This is a concomitant of the ability of organized people at the local level to change their own behavior, to control and manipulate their physical environment, and to redirect social activity, all generally considered to be a fundamental part of, if not a pre-requisite for real development, and appreciated by the political leadership. However, it seemed to be assumed that such processes would be integrally incorporated into government and administrative processes, if allowed to occur at all.

B. Dangers of/to Independent Leadership

A healthy VDO movement should contribute to the emergence of particularly strong, influential individuals outside the context of party or government, or traditional authorities. Unfortunately, in Africa, such individuals usually have come to be considered a threat to higher authority and have been severely constrained, and sometimes imprisoned or even killed. VDO leadership, especially at the level of the
national and international federations of such organizations, are no doubt concerned that they and their work not be associated with that legacy. One can hope that the fact that no one we interviewed saw fit to discuss this issue indicates that it is not (yet?) real.

C. Concern for Environmental Impact of Projects

Generally, it seemed to us that the VDO projects are treated as if, given their small size and localized character, no special attention need be given to their potentially negative impact on the physical environment. Yet, even at the level of an individual project, such as the installation of a well, bore hole, or riverside pump, substantial damage can be done, and has been done. Overgrazing around new water points, and excessive offtake of water from reduced streams and rivers, exacerbation of over-cropping of bio-mass from new or expanded settlements, are not uncommon features of VDO-sponsored projects, just as they are with the larger Government sponsored ones. One should consider, also, the combined impact of hundreds, sometimes thousands, of individual small scale projects. Assessment of the overall combined impact of such projects seems to be missing from the VDO sector, because there is so little coordination of planning and evaluation of the sector by either the VDO community or the government.

D. Documentation and Evaluation

We found little cumulative documentation and assessment of project failure, in order to permit institutional as well as broad social learning from the VDO experience. We found no evidence of an evaluation process that would go much beyond responsible use of funds, or the general achievement or not of the goals of projects. Nor was there much evidence in either the interviews, or documents from the various individual organizations, or the record of the landmark meetings, of a serious application to VDO programs and projects of lessons learned from the long experience of Government and Development Agency-sponsored projects, other than to aim at smaller scale projects that involve and reflect the goals and interests of the local people involved. VDOs are often busy installing equipment that local people have neither the training nor the resources to maintain. They are carrying out single- or limited- sector or issue interventions with people whose needs are complex and multiple.

E. Establishing Large-Scale African Foundations

The opportunity for and benefits of establishing African institutions to collect philanthropically motivated funding from abroad as well as locally, was generally not raised by those we interviewed, in either the government or VDO communities. Yet, a good deal of concern was expressed by both about African institutions being responsible for African development and the consequent need for them to be in charge. The potential for African institutions to establish their own branches in the industrial countries, for their diplomatic communities to be more involved in promoting an under-standing of and use of African institutions and initiatives in fighting drought, famine, poverty and underdevelopment, which we deem to be substantial, seemed not to be visible.

Everywhere it was apparent that great effort was being made to mobilize local resources for combatting the effects of the drought and famine, including the collecting of private contributions from office workers, and the like. But these efforts had not led to the emergence of an institution able and willing to place itself along side of, if not in the place of, the major private international relief and development-promotion agencies, as sources of *funding* and not just training or other servicing of local groups and projects.

VI. Future Imperatives

A. For the Major Finance Sources

1. Donor NGOs: There are sure to be mounting pressures on external donor organizations for longer-term financing commitments coming from host governments as well recipient program VDOs in the field. Donor NGOs will be caught in a squeeze, as public philanthropy diminishes in time, whether from fatigue and saturation with the issue, habituation to the idea of famine

in Africa, or recovery from drought. Yet, the NGOs will know better than most others and feel more committed to the idea that the problems of starvation in Africa are not solved. Creative public education efforts will be required --ones emphasizing the longer term needs and the mutuality of interests involved in promoting genuine development in Africa. The donors may find the need to adopt a multi-year budgeting process, as a standard operating procedure.

2. Development Finance Lenders: As major actors in development policy making as well as a source of advice to African governments on policy, the development finance institutions, such as the international, regional, and national development banks, will be called upon to help mobilize resources of all kinds, not only financial, and beyond their own lending capacities. They are as aware as any of the institutions involved in promoting African development that not all such activity should be financed on a debt-building basis.

B. For African Governments

As African governments carry out decentralization and privatization programs, and experience dwindling resources, pressures to give greater freedom and support to VDOs will grow. There will also be a need to provide infrastructure, fiscal favors, and other supports. Governments will also likely be faced with a need to create or allow new, or modify existing indigenous structures for channeling external VDO assistance, whether in the form of indigenous VDO federations, government monitoring offices, or para-statal institutions.

There is also a great need for understanding of VDO potential and commitment among governmental circles. The African VDO leadership often finds itself balanced on a tightrope, trying to hold up the interest of all of Africa within the world community of non-governmental organizations, where so many plans are made and from which so many resources flow, while keeping out of trouble with officialdom at home. Africa's voice in circles of power within and among external governments and interstate agencies will be faint indeed if intelligent, courageous, experienced and committed Africans dare not assert themselves, become visible leaders, or build strong organizations and programs for constructive action among the people. African VDOs have already emerged as a real factor in the development picture. It remains to be seen if either the external or the internal environments will allow them to remain so.

ACRONYMS

ARD   - Association Régionale de Développement
BFG   - Burkina Faso Government
BSONG   - Bureau de Suivi des Organisations non-Gouvernementales
CCA   - (or CCA-ONG) Comité de Coordination des Actions des
              Organisations non-Gouvernementales
CIDA   - Canadian International Development Agency
CNAVS   - Comité National d'Aide aux Victimes de la Secheresse
CODEL   - Cooperation in Development, Inc. (USA)
CONGAT   - Congress of N.G.O.s in Togo
CRS   - Catholic Relief Service
CWS   - Church World Service
DAC   - Development Assistance Committee (of the O.E.C.D.)
EPI   - Expanded Programs of Immunization
FEME   - Fédération des Églises et Missions Évangéliques
FAVDO   - Federation of African Volunteer Development Org's
GAP   - Grouppement des Aides Privées
GAPVOD   - Ghana Association Private Volunteer Organizations in
              Development
GM   - Grouppement de mutualité (in Niger)
GBF   - Government of Burkina Faso
GOG   - Government of Ghana
GOM   - Government of Mali
GON   - Government of Niger
JOVC   - Japanese Volunteer Service
LA/BA   - Live Aid/Band Aid
MFEP   - Ministry of Finance and Economic Planning
NGO   - Non Governmental Organization
NGLS   - Non Governmental Liaison Service (of United Nations)
OAMES   - Oeuvre Malienne d'Aide à l'Enfance du Sahél (Mali)
OIC   - Opportunities Industrialization Centers
ORD   - Organisation Rurale de Développement
PACT   - Private Agencies Collaborating Together
PAMSCAA-   Program of Action and Measures to Address the Social
              Cost of Adjustment
PDA   - Private Development Agency
PEA   - People's Educational Association (Ghana)
PFP   - Partnership for Productivity
PIP   - Public Investment Program (Ghana)

PNDC	- Provisional National Defense Council (Ghana)
PVO	- Private Voluntary Organization
RDF	- Rural Development Fund (Ghana)
SPONG	- Secrétariat des Organisations non-Gouvernementales
UFN	- Union des Femmes Nigeriènnes
UNDP	- United Nations Development Program
URC	- Unions rurales communautaires (Niger)
USAFA	- United Support of Artists for Africa
USAID	- United States Agency for International Development
VDO	- Volunteer Development Organization

ABOUT THE AUTHORS

Dr. Willard R. Johnson is Professor of Political Science at M.I.T. and, since the early 1970s has directed the <u>Business Management for Economic Development Project</u> at the M.I.T. Center for International Studies (MIT-CIS). He also has directed the Communications Component of the African American Issues Center at the MIT-CIS. During 1987 he was a Fulbright Senior Regional Research Scholar in West Africa.

Dr. Vivian R. Johnson is currently an Associate Professor of Education at the Boston University Graduate School of Education. She is also Research Director of the Institute for Responsive Education in Boston. From 1980-1986, she was Campus Coordinator for Boston University School of Medicine's "Project for Strengthening Health Delivery Systems in Africa", a field-headquartered project that sponsored training in twenty West and Central African countries.

The Business Management for Economic Development Project, under the auspicies of which this study was issued as a monograph in 1988, attempts to assess efforts of and opportunities for directly productive organizations, especially international businesses and regional as well as international development finance institutions, to maximize their external contributions to the general development of their host economies while satisfying their own internal requirements. Other studies published by and available from this project include:

--W.R. Johnson, "Training Business Managers to Promote Economic Development." 1974. 42p.

--W.R. Johnson, "International Investment and the Transfer of Power." 1974. 37p.

--C.A. Bloomberg, "The Transfer of Management Technology in the Commonwealth Development Corporation." 1974. 36p. and Postscript by W.R. Johnson.

--J.G. Karuga, "Africanization and Management Development in Kenya." 1974. 38p. and Postscript by W.R. Johnson.

--M.M. Toby and W.R. Johnson, "The Commonwealth Development Corporation's Contribution to Housing Development: A Case Study from Kenya." 1975. 84p. and Supplement by authors and by the C.D.C.

--W.R. Johnson, "The Potential Role of African Development Banks in the Creation of African Owned and Managed General Management Services Corporations." 1976. 26p.

--W.R. Johnson, "African, Arab, Western Industrial Country Tri-lateral Cooperation: A Note of Caution." 1978. 20p.

--W.R. Johnson, "How Long Africa's Dependency?" 1983. 23p.